An Enemy of the People
Original English Translation
(1882)

Henrik Ibsen
Translated by:
Mrs. E. Marx-Aveling

HENRIK IBSEN
(1828 – 1906)

An Enemy of the People

Henrik Ibsen

Characters.

———◆———

DOCTOR THOMAS STOCKMANN, *medical officer of the Baths.*
MRS. STOCKMANN, *his wife.*
PETRA, *their daughter, a teacher.*
EILIF, } *their sons, boys of thirteen.*
MORTEN, }
PETER STOCKMANN, *the doctor's elder brother, Burgomaster[1] and chief*
  of police, chairman of the Baths Committee, etc.
MORTEN KIIL, *master tanner, Mrs. Stockmann's foster-father*
HOVSTAD, *editor of the " People's Messenger."*
BILLING, *on the staff.*
HORSTER, *a ship's captain.*
ASLAKSEN, *a printer.*

Townsfolk present at the meeting ; all sorts and conditions of men, some
women, and a flock of school-boys.

SCENE : *A town on the South Coast of Norway.*

---

[1] "Burgomaster" is the most convenient substitute for "Byfogd," but
"Town Clerk" would perhaps be a nearer approach to a literal rendering of the
term. It is impossible to find exact counterparts in English for the different
grades of the Norwegian bureaucracy.

AN ENEMY OF THE PEOPLE.

PLAY IN FIVE ACTS.

———•◦•———

Act First.

(*Evening.* DR. STOCKMANN'S *sitting-room; simply but neatly fitted and furnished. In the wall to the right are two doors, the first leading to the Doctor's study, the second to an anteroom. In the opposite wall, facing the anteroom door, a door leading to the other rooms. Near the middle of this wall stands the stove; further towards the foreground a sofa, with a mirror above it, and in front of it an oval table with a cover. On the table a lighted lamp, with a shade. In the back wall an open door leading to the dining-room, in which is seen a supper-table, with a lamp on it.*)

(BILLING *is seated at the table, a napkin under his chin. MRS. STOCKMANN stands by the table and hands him a plate with a large slice of roast beef. The other seats round the table are empty; the table is in disorder, as after a meal.*)

MRS. STOCKMANN. Well, if you're an hour late, Mr. Billing, you must put up with a cold supper.

BILLING (*eating*). It's excellent, delicious!

MRS. STOCKMANN. You know how Stockmann insists on regular meal-hours——

BILLING. Oh, I don't mind at all. I almost think it tastes better when I can sit down like this and have it all to myself, undisturbed.

MRS. STOCKMANN. Well, if you're satisfied——
(*Listening in the direction of the anteroom.*) Surely
that's Hovstad coming too.

BILLING. Very likely.

(BURGOMASTER STOCKMANN *enters, wearing an
overcoat and an official gold-laced cap, and carry-
ing a stick.*)

BURGOMASTER. Good evening, sister-in-law.

MRS. STOCKMANN (*coming into the sitting-room*).
Oh, good evening; is it you? It's very nice of you
to look in.

BURGOMASTER. I was just passing, and so——
(*Looks towards the dining-room.*) Ah! I see you have
company.

MRS. STOCKMANN (*rather embarrassed*). Oh, no!
Not at all; it's the merest chance. (*Hurriedly.*)
Won't you come and have something?

BURGOMASTER. I? No, thanks. Good gracious!
hot meat in the evening! that wouldn't suit *my*
digestion.

MRS. STOCKMANN. Oh! for once in a way——

BURGOMASTER. No, no. Much obliged to you.
I stick to tea and bread and butter. It's more
wholesome in the long run—and rather more
economical, too.

MRS. STOCKMANN (*smiling*). You mustn't think
Thomas and I are mere spendthrifts, either.

BURGOMASTER. You're not, sister-in-law; far be
it from me to say that. (*Pointing to the Doctor's
study.*) Is he not at home?

MRS. STOCKMANN. No, he's gone for a little turn
after supper—with the boys.

BURGOMASTER. I wonder if that's good for him? (*Listening.*) There he is.

MRS. STOCKMANN. No, that's not he. (*A knock.*) Come in! (HOVSTAD *enters from the anteroom.*) Ah! it's Mr. Hovstad——

HOVSTAD. You must excuse me; I was detained at the printer's. Good evening, Burgomaster.

BURGOMASTER (*bowing rather stiffly*). Mr. Hovstad! Come on business, I presume?

HOVSTAD. Partly. About something for the paper.

BURGOMASTER. So I supposed. I hear my brother's an extremely prolific contributor to the *People's Messenger.*

HOVSTAD. Yes, he's good enough to give the *Messenger* the benefit when he wants to relieve his mind on any special subject.

MRS. STOCKMANN (*to* HOVSTAD). But won't you——? (*Points to the dining-room.*)

BURGOMASTER. God forbid I should blame him for writing for the class of readers he finds most in sympathy with him. And, personally, I've no reason to bear your paper any ill-will, Mr. Hovstad.

HOVSTAD. No, I should think not.

BURGOMASTER. On the whole, there's a great deal of mutual toleration in our town;—an excellent public spirit. And that's because we have a great common interest to hold us together—an interest in which all right-minded citizens are equally concerned.

HOVSTAD. Yes—the Baths.

BURGOMASTER. Just so. We have our magnificent new Baths. You'll see! The whole life of the town will centre around the Baths, Mr. Hovstad, beyond a doubt !

MRS. STOCKMANN. That's just what Thomas says.

BURGOMASTER. How marvellously the place has developed, even within the last few years. Money has come into circulation, and brought life and movement with it. Houses and ground-rents rise in value every day.

HOVSTAD. And the difficulty of getting work is decreasing.

BURGOMASTER. That's true. There's a gratifying diminution in the burden imposed on the well-to-do classes by the poor-rates ; and they will be still further lightened if only we have a really good summer this year—plenty of visitors—lots of invalids, to give the Baths a reputation.

HOVSTAD. I hear there's every prospect of that.

BURGOMASTER. Things look most promising. Inquiries about apartments and so forth are flowing in every day.

HOVSTAD. Then the Doctor's paper will come in very opportunely.

BURGOMASTER. Has he been writing again ?

HOVSTAD. It's a thing he wrote in the winter ; eulogising the Baths, and enlarging on the excellent sanitary conditions of the town. But at the time I held it over.

BURGOMASTER. Ha! I suppose there was some little hitch.

HOVSTAD. Not at all. But I thought it better to keep it till the spring, when people are beginning to look about them, and think of their summer quarters.

BURGOMASTER. You're right, quite right, Mr. Hovstad.

MRS. STOCKMANN. Yes, Thomas is really indefatigable where the Baths are concerned.

BURGOMASTER. Well, you know, he's one of the staff.

HOVSTAD. And of course he was really their creator.

BURGOMASTER. Was he? I hear now and then that certain persons are of that opinion. But I should have thought that I too had a modest share in that undertaking.

MRS. STOCKMANN. Yes, that's what Thomas is always saying.

HOVSTAD. Who wants to deny it, Burgomaster? You set the thing going, and put it on a practical footing; everybody knows that. I only meant that the original idea was the doctor's.

BURGOMASTER. Yes, my brother has certainly had ideas enough in his time—worse luck! But when it comes to realising them, Mr. Hovstad, we want men of another stamp. I should have expected that in this house at least——

MRS. STOCKMANN. Why, my dear brother-in-law——

HOVSTAD. Burgomaster, how can you——?

MRS. STOCKMANN. Do go in and take something, Mr. Hovstad; my husband is sure to be in directly.

HOVSTAD. Thanks; just a mouthful, perhaps.

(*He goes into the dining-room.*)

BURGOMASTER (*speaking in a low voice*). It's

extraordinary how people who spring directly from the peasant-class never can get rid of a want of tact.

MRS. STOCKMANN.   But why should you care? Can't you and Thomas share the honour, like brothers?

BURGOMASTER.   Yes, one would suppose so; but it seems a share of the honour isn't enough for some persons.

MRS. STOCKMANN.   What nonsense!   You and Thomas always get on so well together.   (*Listening.*) There, I think I hear him.

(*Goes and opens the door of the anteroom.*)

DR. STOCKMANN (*laughing and talking loudly without*).   Here's another visitor for you, Katrine. Isn't it jolly, eh?   Come in, Captain Horster.   Hang your coat on that peg.   What! you don't wear an overcoat?   Fancy, Katrine, I caught him in the street, and I could hardly get him to come along. (CAPTAIN HORSTER *enters and bows to* MRS. STOCK-MANN. *The* DOCTOR *is by the door.*)   In with you, boys.   They're famished again!   Come on, Captain; you must have some of our roast beef——

(*He forces* HORSTER *into the dining-room.* EILIF *and* MORTEN *join them.*)

MRS. STOCKMANN. But, Thomas, don't you see——

DR. STOCKMANN (*turning round in the doorway*). Oh! is that you, Peter?   (*Goes up to him and holds out his hand.*)   Now this is really jolly.

BURGOMASTER.   Unfortunately, I must be off directly——

DR. STOCKMANN.   Nonsense!   We'll have some

toddy in a minute. You're not forgetting the toddy, Katrine?

MRS. STOCKMANN. Of course not; the water's boiling.

(*She goes into the dining-room.*)

BURGOMASTER. Toddy too——!

DR. STOCKMANN. Yes; sit down, and let's enjoy ourselves.

BURGOMASTER. Thanks; I never join in drinking-parties.

DR. STOCKMANN. But this isn't a party.

BURGOMASTER. It seems to me—— (*Looks towards the dining-room.*) It's wonderful how they can get through all that food.

DR. STOCKMANN (*rubbing his hands*). Yes, doesn't it do one good to see young people eat? Always hungry! That's as it should be! They must eat. They need strength! It's they that have got to keep the ferment of the future astir, Peter.

BURGOMASTER. May I ask what there is to be "kept astir," as you call it?

DR. STOCKMANN. You'll have to ask the young people that—when the time comes. *We* shan't see it, of course. Two old fogies like you and me——

BURGOMASTER. Come, come—surely that's a very extraordinary expression to use——

DR. STOCKMANN. Oh, you mustn't mind my nonsense, Peter. I'm in glorious spirits, you see. I feel so unspeakably happy in the midst of all this growing, germinating life. After all, what a glorious time we live in! It seems as though a whole new world were springing up around us.

BURGOMASTER. Do you really think so?

DR. STOCKMANN. Of course you can't see it as clearly as I do. You've passed your life in the midst of it all; and that deadens the impression. But I, who had to vegetate all those years in that little hole in the north, hardly ever seeing a soul that could speak a stimulating word to me—all this affects me as if I had suddenly dropped into the heart of some great metropolis——

BURGOMASTER. Hm ; metropolis——

DR. STOCKMANN. Oh! I know well enough that things are on a small scale here compared with many other places. But there's vitality and promise—an infinity of things to work and strive for; and that's the main point. (*Calling.*) Katrine, haven't there been any letters?

MRS. STOCKMANN (*in the dining-room*). No, none at all.

DR. STOCKMANN. And then a good income, Peter! That's a thing one learns to appreciate when one has lived on starvation wages——

BURGOMASTER. Good heavens——!

DR. STOCKMANN. Oh yes! I can tell you we had often hard times of it up there. And now we can live like princes! To-day, for example, we had roast beef for dinner, and we've had some of it for supper too. Won't you have some! Come along—just look at it, anyhow.

BURGOMASTER. No no ; certainly not——

DR. STOCKMANN. Well then, look here. Do you see we've bought a table-cover?

BURGOMASTER. Yes, so I observed.

DR. STOCKMANN. And a lamp-shade too. Do
you see? Katrine has been saving up for them.
They make the room look comfortable, don't they?
Come over here. No no no, not there! So—yes—
do you see what a rich light it throws down?—I
really think it looks very nice. Eh?

BURGOMASTER. Yes, when one can afford such
luxuries——

DR. STOCKMANN. Oh yes, I can afford it now.
Katrine says I make almost as much as we spend.

BURGOMASTER. Yes—almost!

DR. STOCKMANN. Besides, a man of science must
live in some style. Why, I believe a mere sheriff[1]
spends much more a year than I do.

BURGOMASTER. Yes, I daresay! A member of
the superior magistracy!

DR. STOCKMANN. Well then, even a common
merchant! A man of that sort will get through
many times as much——

BURGOMASTER. That's natural, in your relative
positions——

DR. STOCKMANN. And, after all, I really don't
spend anything unnecessarily, Peter. But I can't deny
myself the delight of having people about me. I must
have them. After being so long isolated, I find it
a necessity of life to have bright, cheerful, freedom-
loving, hard-working young men around me—and
that's what they are, all of them, sitting there eating
so heartily. I wish you knew more of Hovstad——

BURGOMASTER. Ah, Hovstad! He was telling

---

[1] *Amtmand*, the chief official of an *Amt* or county; consequently a
high dignitary in the bureaucratic hierarchy.

me that he's going to publish another article of yours.

DR. STOCKMANN.   An article of mine?

BURGOMASTER.   Yes, about the Baths.   An article you wrote last winter——

DR. STOCKMANN.   Oh, that one!   But I don't want that to appear just now.

BURGOMASTER.   Why not?   It seems to me this is the very time for it.

DR. STOCKMANN.   Very likely—under ordinary circumstances—— (*Crosses the room.*)

BURGOMASTER (*looking after him*).   And what's unusual in the circumstances now?

DR. STOCKMANN (*standing still*).   Peter, I really can't tell you yet—not this evening, at all events. There may prove to be a great deal that's unusual in the circumstances.   On the other hand, there may be nothing at all.   Very likely it's only my fancy.

BURGOMASTER.   Upon my word, you're very enigmatical.   Is there anything in the wind?   Anything I'm to be kept in the dark about?   I should think, as Chairman of the Bath Committee——

DR. STOCKMANN.   And I should think that I—— There! don't let's get our backs up, Peter.

BURGOMASTER.   God forbid!   I'm not in the habit of "getting my back up," as you express it. But I must absolutely insist that everything shall be carried on in a business-like manner, and through the proper authorities.   I can't be a party to crooked or underhand ways.

DR. STOCKMANN.   Have *I* ever been given to crooked or underhand ways?

BURGOMASTER. Anyhow, you have an ingrained propensity to going your own way. And that, in a well-ordered community, is almost as inadmissible. The individual must submit to society, or, more precisely, to the authorities whose business it is to watch over the welfare of society.

DR. STOCKMANN. Maybe. But what the devil has that to do with me?

BURGOMASTER. Why that's the very thing, my dear Thomas, that it seems you won't learn. But take care; you'll have to pay for it sooner or later. Now I've warned you. Good-bye.

DR. STOCKMANN. Are you quite mad? You're on a totally wrong track——

BURGOMASTER. I'm not usually on the wrong track. Besides, I must beg you not to—— (*Bowing towards dining-room.*) Good-bye, sister-in-law; good-bye, gentlemen.

(*He goes.*)

MRS. STOCKMANN (*entering the sitting-room*). Is he gone?

DR. STOCKMANN. Yes, and in a fine temper, too.

MRS. STOCKMANN. Why, my dear Thomas, what have you been saying to him now?

DR. STOCKMANN. Nothing at all. He can't expect me to account to him for everything—before the time comes.

MRS. STOCKMANN. What are you to account to him for?

DR. STOCKMANN. Hm! Never mind about that, Katrine. It's very odd that there are no letters.

(HOVSTAD, BILLING, *and* HORSTER *have risen from table and come forward into the sitting-room.* EILIF *and* MORTEN *presently follow.*)

BILLING (*stretching himself*). Ah! Strike me dead if one doesn't feel a new man after such a meal.

HOVSTAD. The Burgomaster didn't seem in the best of tempers this evening.

DR. STOCKMANN. That's his stomach. He has a very poor digestion.

HOVSTAD. It's the staff of the *Messenger* he finds it hardest to stomach.

MRS. STOCKMANN. I thought you got on with him well enough.

HOVSTAD. Oh, yes! But it's only a sort of armistice between us.

BILLING. That's it. That word sums up the situation.

DR. STOCKMANN. We must remember that Peter's a bachelor, poor devil! He has no home to be happy in ; only business, business. And then all that cursed weak tea he goes and pours down his throat! Now then, put chairs round the table, boys! Katrine, shan't we have the toddy now?

MRS. STOCKMANN (*going towards the dining-room*). I'm just getting it.

DR. STOCKMANN. And you, Captain Horster, sit down by me on the sofa. So rare a guest as you—— Be seated, gentlemen.

(*The men sit round the table;* MRS. STOCKMANN *brings in a tray with kettle, glasses, decanters, etc.*)

MRS. STOCKMANN. There you are! Here's arrak, and this is rum, and this cognac. Now, help yourselves.

DR. STOCKMANN (*taking a glass*). So we will! (*While the toddy is being mixed.*) And now out with the cigars. Eilif, I'm sure you know where the box is. And you, Morten, may fetch my pipe. (*The boys go into the room, right.*) I have a suspicion that Eilif cribs a cigar now and then, but I pretend not to notice it. (*Calls.*) And my smoking-cap, Morten. Katrine, can't you tell him where I left it? Ah! he's got it. (*The boys bring in the things.*) Now, friends, help yourselves. You know I stick to my pipe;—this one has been on many a stormy journey with me, up there in the north. (*They clink glasses.*) Your health! Ah, I can tell you it's better fun to sit cosily here, safe from wind and weather.

MRS. STOCKMANN (*who sits knitting*). Do you sail soon, Captain Horster?

HORSTER. I hope to be ready for a start by next week.

MRS. STOCKMANN. And you're going to America?

HORSTER. Yes, that's the intention.

BILLING. But then you'll miss the election of the new Town Council.

HORSTER. Is there to be an election again?

BILLING. Didn't you know?

HORSTER. No, I don't bother about these things.

BILLING. But I suppose you take an interest in public affairs?

HORSTER. No, I don't understand anything about them.

BILLING. Still one ought to make use of one's vote.

HORSTER. Even those who don't understand anything about it?

BILLING. Understand? Now, what do you mean by that? Society's like a ship: every man must put his hand to the helm.

HORSTER. That may be all right on shore; but at sea it wouldn't do at all.

HOVSTAD. It's remarkable how little sailors care about public affairs, as a rule.

BILLING. Most extraordinary.

DR. STOCKMANN. Sailors are like birds of passage: they're at home both in the south and in the north. So the rest of us have to be all the more energetic, Mr. Hovstad. Will there be anything of public interest in the *People's Messenger* to-morrow?

HOVSTAD. Nothing of local interest. But the day after to-morrow I'm thinking of printing your article——

DR. STOCKMANN. Oh confound it, I say! You'll have to hold that over.

HOVSTAD. Really? We happen to have plenty of space, and I should say this was the very time for it——

DR. STOCKMANN. Yes yes, you may be right, but you'll have to hold it over all the same. I'll explain to you by-and-by——

(PETRA, *wearing a hat and cloak, and with a number of exercise books under her arm, comes in from the anteroom.*)

PETRA. Good evening!

DR. STOCKMANN. Good evening, Petra! Is that you?

(*General greetings.* PETRA *puts her cloak, hat, and books on a chair by the door.*)

PETRA. Here you all are, enjoying yourselves, while I've been out slaving!

DR. STOCKMANN. Well then, you come and enjoy yourself too.

BILLING. May I mix you a little——?

PETRA (*coming towards the table*). Thanks, I'll help myself—you always make it too strong. But, by the way, father, I've a letter for you.

(*Goes to the chair where her things are lying.*)

DR. STOCKMANN. A letter! From whom?

PETRA (*searching in the pocket of her cloak*). I got it from the postman just as I was going out——

DR. STOCKMANN (*rising and going towards her*). And you only bring it me now?

PETRA. I really hadn't time to run up again. Here it is.

DR. STOCKMANN (*seizing the letter*). Let me see, let me see, child. (*Reads the address.*) Yes; that's it——

MRS. STOCKMANN. Is it the one you've been expecting so, Thomas?

DR. STOCKMANN. Yes, it is. I must go at once—— Where shall I find a light, Katrine? Is there no lamp in my study again?

MRS. STOCKMANN. Yes—the lamp's lit. It's on the writing-table.

DR. STOCKMANN. Good. Excuse me one mo-ment——

(*He goes into the room on the right.*)

PETRA. What can it be, mother?

MRS. STOCKMANN. I don't know. For the last few days he's been continually on the look-out for the postman.

BILLING. Probably a country patient——

PETRA. Poor father! He'll soon have far too much to do. (*Mixes her toddy.*) Ah! this'll be good.

HOVSTAD. Have you been teaching in the night school as well to-day?

PETRA (*sipping her glass*). Two hours.

BILLING. And four hours in the morning at the institute——

PETRA (*sitting down by the table*). Five hours.

MRS. STOCKMANN. And I see you've some exercises to correct this evening.

PETRA. Yes, a heap of them.

HORSTER. It seems to me you've plenty to do, too.

PETRA. Yes; but I like it. One feels so delightfully tired after it.

BILLING. Do you like that?

PETRA. Yes, for then one sleeps so well.

MORTEN. I say, Petra, you must be a great sinner.

PETRA. A sinner!

MORTEN. Yes, if you work so hard. Mr. Rörlund[1] says work is a punishment for our sins.

EILIF (*contemptuously*). Bosh! What a silly you are to believe such stuff as that!

MRS. STOCKMANN. Come come, Eilif.

BILLING (*laughing*). Capital, capital!

[1] See *The Pillars of Society*.

HOVSTAD. Wouldn't you like to work so hard, Morten?

MORTEN. No, I shouldn't.

HOVSTAD. What do you intend to be, then?

MORTEN. I should like to be a Viking.

EILIF. But then you'd have to be a heathen.

MORTEN. Well, so I would.

BILLING. There I agree with you, Morten. I say just the same.

MRS. STOCKMANN (*making a sign to him*). No, no, Mr. Billing, you don't.

BILLING. Strike me dead but I do, though. I *am* a heathen, and I'm proud of it. You'll see we shall all be heathens soon.

MORTEN. And shall we be able to do anything we like then?

BILLING. Well, you see, Morten——

MRS. STOCKMANN. Now run away, boys; I'm sure you've some lessons to prepare for to-morrow.

EILIF. You might let me stay just a little longer——

MRS. STOCKMANN. No, you must go too. Be off, both of you.

(*The boys say good-night and go into the room on the left.*)

HOVSTAD. Do you really think it can hurt the boys to hear these things?

MRS. STOCKMANN. Well, I don't know; but I don't like it.

PETRA. Well mother, I think you're quite wrong there.

MRS. STOCKMANN.   Maybe!   But I don't like it—here, at home.

PETRA.   There's no end of hypocrisy both at home and at school.   At home you must hold your tongue, and at school you have to stand up and lie to the children.

HORSTER.   To lie?

PETRA.   Yes; do you think we don't have to teach many and many a thing we don't believe ourselves?

BILLING.   Yes, we know that well enough.

PETRA.   If only I could afford it, I'd start a school myself, and things should be very different there.

BILLING.   Oh, afford it——!

HORSTER.   If you're really thinking of doing that, Miss Stockmann, I shall be delighted to let you have a room at my place.   My father's old house is nearly empty; there's a large dining-room on the ground floor——

PETRA (*laughing*).   Oh, thank you very much—but nothing will come of it.

HOVSTAD.   Oh no!   I fancy Miss Petra will rather go in for journalism.   By the way, have you had time to look into the English novel you promised to translate for us——?

PETRA.   Not yet.   But you shall have it in good time.

(DR. STOCKMANN *enters from his room, with the letter open in his hand.*)

DR. STOCKMANN (*flourishing the letter*).   Here's news, I can tell you, that'll wake up the town!

BILLING.   News?

MRS. STOCKMANN.   What news?

DR. STOCKMANN. A great discovery, Katrine.

HOVSTAD. What?

MRS. STOCKMANN. Made by you?

DR. STOCKMANN. Yes—by me! (*Walks up and down.*) *Now* let them go on accusing me of fads and crack-brained notions. But they'll not dare to. Ha-ha! I know they won't.

PETRA. Father, do tell us what it is.

DR. STOCKMANN. Well well, give me time, and you shall hear all about it. If only Peter were here now! This just shows how we men can go about forming judgments like the blindest moles——

HOVSTAD. What do you mean, doctor?

DR. STOCKMANN (*standing beside the table*). Isn't it generally supposed that our town is healthy?

HOVSTAD. Of course.

DR. STOCKMANN. Indeed a quite exceptionally healthy place,—a place to be confidently recommended, both to invalids and people in health——

MRS. STOCKMANN. My dear Thomas——

DR. STOCKMANN. And certainly we haven't failed to recommend and belaud it. I've written again and again, both in the *Messenger* and in pamphlets——

HOVSTAD. Well, what then?

DR. STOCKMANN. These Baths, that we've called the pulse of the town, its spinal nerve, and—and the devil knows what else——

BILLING. "The town's palpitating heart," I was once moved to call them in a convivial moment——

DR. STOCKMANN. Yes, I daresay. But do you know what they really are, these mighty, magnificent, belauded Baths, that have cost so much money—do you know what they are?

HOVSTAD. No, what are they?

MRS. STOCKMANN. Do tell us.

DR. STOCKMANN. Simply a pestiferous hole.

PETRA. The Baths, father?

MRS. STOCKMANN (*at the same time*). Our Baths!

HOVSTAD (*also at the same time*). But, Doctor——!

BILLING. Oh, it's incredible!

DR. STOCKMANN. I tell you the whole place is a poisonous whited-sepulchre; noxious in the highest degree! All that filth up there in the Mill Dale, with its horrible stench, taints the water in the feed-pipes of the Baths; and the same confounded poisonous refuse oozes out by the beach——

HOVSTAD. Where the sea-baths are?

DR. STOCKMANN. Exactly.

HOVSTAD. But how are you so sure of all this, Doctor?

DR. STOCKMANN. I've investigated the whole thing as conscientiously as possible. I've long had my doubts about it. Last year we had some extraordinary cases of illness among the patients—both typhoid and gastric attacks——

MRS. STOCKMANN. Yes, I remember.

DR. STOCKMANN. At the time we thought the visitors had brought the infection with them; but afterwards—last winter—I began to question that. So I set about testing the water as well as I could.

MRS. STOCKMANN. It was that you were working so hard at!

DR. STOCKMANN. Yes, you may well say I've

worked, Katrine. But here, you know, I hadn't the necessary scientific appliances; so I sent samples both of our drinking-water and of our sea-water to the University for exact analysis by a chemist.

HOVSTAD. And you've received his report?

DR. STOCKMANN (*showing letter*). Here it is. And it proves beyond dispute the presence of putrifying organic matter in the water—millions of infusoria. It's absolutely noxious to health, whether used internally or externally.

MRS. STOCKMANN. What a blessing you found it out in time!

DR. STOCKMANN. Yes, you may well say that.

HOVSTAD. And what do you intend to do now, Doctor?

DR. STOCKMANN. Why, to set things right, of course.

HOVSTAD. Do you think that can be done?

DR. STOCKMANN. It must be done. Else the whole Baths are useless, ruined. But there's no fear. I'm quite clear as to what is required.

MRS. STOCKMANN. But, my dear Thomas, why should you have made such a secret of all this?

DR. STOCKMANN. Would you have had me rush all over the town and chatter about it before I was quite certain? No, thanks! I'm not so mad as that.

PETRA. But to us at home——

DR. STOCKMANN. I couldn't say a word to a living soul. But to-morrow you may look in at the Badger's——

MRS. STOCKMANN. Oh, Thomas!

DR. STOCKMANN. Well well, at your grandfather's. The old fellow *will* be astonished! He thinks I'm not quite right in my head—yes, and plenty of others think the same, I've noticed. But now these good people shall see—yes, they shall see now! (*Walks up and down rubbing his hands.*) What a stir there'll be in the town, Katrine! Just think of it! All the water-pipes will have to be re-laid.

HOVSTAD (*rising*). All the water-pipes?

DR. STOCKMANN. Why, of course. The intake is too low down; it must be moved much higher up.

PETRA. So you were right, after all.

DR. STOCKMANN. Yes, do you remember, Petra? I wrote against it when they were beginning the works. But then no one would listen to me. Now, you may be sure, I'll give them my full broadside— for of course I've prepared a statement for the Directors; it's been lying there ready a whole week; I've only been waiting for this report. (*Points to letter.*) But now they shall have it at once. (*Goes into his room and returns with a packet of papers.*) See! Four closely-written sheets. And I'll enclose the report. A newspaper, Katrine! Get me something to wrap them up in. There—that's· it. Give it to— to—— (*Stamps.*) What the devil's her name? Give it to the girl, I mean, and tell her to take it at once to the Burgomaster.

(MRS. STOCKMANN *goes out with packet through the dining-room.*)

PETRA. What do you think Uncle Peter will say, father?

DR. STOCKMANN. What should he say? He's

bound to be pleased at the discovery of so important a fact.

HOVSTAD. I suppose you'll let me put a short notice of your discovery in the *Messenger*.

DR. STOCKMANN. Yes, I shall be very glad if you will.

HOVSTAD. It's highly desirable that the public should know about it as soon as possible.

DR. STOCKMANN. Yes, certainly.

MRS. STOCKMANN (*returning*). She's gone with it.

BILLING. Strike me dead if you won't be the first man in the town, Doctor.

DR. STOCKMANN (*walks up and down in high glee*). Oh, nonsense! After all, I've done no more than my duty. I've been a lucky treasure-hunter, that's all. But all the same——

BILLING. Hovstad, don't you think the town ought to do homage to, Dr. Stockmann in a torch-light procession?

HOVSTAD. I shall certainly propose it.

BILLING. And I'll talk it over with Aslaksen.

DR. STOCKMANN. No, dear friends; let all such claptrap alone. I won't hear of anything of the sort. And if the Directors want to raise my salary, I won't accept it. I tell you, Katrine, I will not accept it.

MRS. STOCKMANN. Quite right, Thomas.

PETRA (*raising her glass*). Your health, father.

HOVSTAD *and* BILLING. Your health, your health, Doctor!

HORSTER (*touching glasses with the* DOCTOR). I wish you nothing but joy of your discovery.

DR. STOCKMANN. Thanks, thanks, my dear

friends. I can't tell you how happy I am——! Oh, what a blessing it is to feel that you've deserved well of your native town and your fellow-citizens. Hurrah, Katrine!

 (He puts both his arms round her neck, and whirls her round with him. MRS. STOCKMANN *screams and struggles. A burst of laughter, applause, and cheers for the* DOCTOR. *The boys thrust their heads in at the door.)*

Act Second.

(*The* DOCTOR'S *sitting-room. The dining-room door is closed. Morning.*)

MRS. STOCKMANN (*enters from the dining-room with a sealed letter in her hand, goes to the first door on the right, and peeps in*).   Are you there, Thomas?

DR. STOCKMANN (*within*).   Yes, I've just come in. (*Enters.*)   What is it?

MRS. STOCKMANN.   A letter from your brother.
(*Hands him the letter.*)

DR. STOCKMANN.   Ah! let's see.   (*Opens the envelope and reads.*)   "The MS. sent me is returned herewith——"   (*Reads on, muttering.*)   Hm——!

MRS. STOCKMANN.   Well, what does he say?

DR. STOCKMANN (*putting the paper in his pocket*). Nothing;   only that he'll   come   up   himself   about mid-day.

MRS. STOCKMANN.   Then be sure you remember to stop at home.

DR. STOCKMANN.   Oh, I can easily manage that; I've finished my morning's work.

MRS. STOCKMANN.   I'm   very   curious   to   know how he takes it.

DR. STOCKMANN.   You'll   see   he   won't   be   over pleased that it's I, and not he himself, that have made the discovery.

VOL. II.   9

Mrs. Stockmann.   Ah, that's just what I'm afraid of.

Dr. Stockmann.   Of course at bottom he'll be glad.   But still—Peter is damnably unwilling that any one but himself should do anything for the good of the town.

Mrs. Stockmann.   Do you know, Thomas, I think you might stretch a point, and share the honour with him.   Couldn't you make out that it was he that put you on the track——?

Dr. Stockmann.   By all means, for aught I care. If only I can get things put straight, I——

(*Old* Morten Kiil *peeps in through the anteroom door, looks round inquiringly, and asks slyly.*)

Morten Kiil.   Is it—is it true?

Mrs. Stockmann (*going towards him*).   Father, is that you?

Dr. Stockmann.   Hallo, father-in-law! good morning, good morning.

Mrs. Stockmann.   But do come in.

Morten Kiil. Yes, if it's true; if not, I'm off again.

Dr. Stockmann.   If what is true?

Morten Kiil.   This business about the water-works.   Now, *is* it true?

Dr. Stockmann.   Why, of course it is.   But how did you come to hear of it.

Morten Kiil (*coming in*).   Petra looked in on her way to the school——

Dr. Stockmann.   Oh, did she?

Morten Kiil.   Ay ay—and she told me—— I thought she was only making game of me ; but that's not like Petra either.

DR. STOCKMANN. No, indeed; how could you think so?

MORTEN KIIL. Oh, you can never be sure of anybody. You may be made a fool of before you know where you are. So it is true, after all?

DR. STOCKMANN. · Most certainly it is. Do sit down, father-in-law. (*Forces him down on the sofa.*) Now isn't it a real blessing for the town——?

MORTEN KIIL (*suppressing his laughter*). A blessing for the town?

DR. STOCKMANN. Yes, that I made the discovery in time——

MORTEN KIIL (*as before*). Yes yes yes; but I could never have believed you'd have played your very own brother such a trick.

DR. STOCKMANN. Such a trick!

MRS. STOCKMANN. Oh, my dear father——

MORTEN KIIL (*resting his hands and chin on the top of his stick and winking slyly at the* DOCTOR). What was it again? Wasn't it that some animals had got into the water-pipes?

DR. STOCKMANN. Yes; infusorial animals.

MORTEN KIIL. And any number of these animals had got in, Petra said; an enormous lot.

DR. STOCKMANN. Certainly; hundreds of thousands of them.

MORTEN KIIL. But no one can see them—isn't that so?

DR. STOCKMANN. Quite right; no one can see them.

MORTEN KIIL (*with a quiet, chuckling laugh*). I'll be damned if that isn't the best thing I've heard of you yet.

DR. STOCKMANN. What do you mean?

MORTEN KIIL. But you'll never in this world make the Burgomaster take in anything of the sort.

DR. STOCKMANN. Well, that we'll see.

MORTEN KIIL. Do you really think he'll be so crazy?

DR. STOCKMANN. I hope the whole town will be so crazy.

MORTEN KIIL. The whole town! Well, I don't say but it may. But it serves them right; it'll teach them a lesson. They wanted to be so much cleverer than we old fellows. They hounded me out of the Town Council. Yes; I tell you they hounded me out like a dog, that they did. But now it's their turn. Just you keep up the game with them, Stockmann.

DR. STOCKMANN. Yes, but, father-in-law——

MORTEN KIIL. Keep it up, I say. (*Rising.*) If you can make the Burgomaster and his friends swallow all that, I'll give a hundred crowns straight away to the poor.

DR. STOCKMANN. That's good of you.

MORTEN KIIL. Of course I've little enough to throw away; but if you manage that, I'll certainly give the poor fifty crowns at Christmas.

(HOVSTAD *enters from anteroom.*)

HOVSTAD. Good morning! (*Pausing.*) Oh! I beg your pardon——

DR. STOCKMANN. Not at all. Come in, come in.

MORTEN KIIL (*chuckling again*). He! Is he in it too?

HOVSTAD. What do you mean?

DR. STOCKMANN. Yes, of course he's in it.

MORTEN KIIL. I might have known it! It's to go into the papers. Ah! you're the one, Stockmann! Think of what I've been saying. Now I'm off.

DR. STOCKMANN. Oh no! Stop a little, father-in-law.

MORTEN KIIL. No, I'm off now. Play them all the tricks you can. Deuce take me but you shan't lose by it.

(*He goes,* MRS. STOCKMANN *accompanying him.*)

DR. STOCKMANN (*laughing*). What do you think——? The old fellow doesn't believe a word of all this about the water-works.

HOVSTAD. Was that what he——?

DR. STOCKMANN. Yes; that was what we were talking about. And perhaps you've come on the same business?

HOVSTAD. Yes. Have you a moment to spare, Doctor?

DR. STOCKMANN. As many as you like, my dear fellow.

HOVSTAD. Have you heard anything from the Burgomaster?

DR. STOCKMANN. Not yet. He'll be here presently.

HOVSTAD. I've been thinking over the matter since last evening.

DR. STOCKMANN. Well——?

HOVSTAD. To you, as a doctor and a man of science, this business of the water-works is an isolated affair. I fancy it hasn't occurred to you that a good many other things are bound up with it?

DR. STOCKMANN. Yes?—how? Let's sit down, my dear fellow. No—there, on the sofa.

(HOVSTAD *sits on sofa; the* DOCTOR *in an easy-chair on the other side of the table.*)

DR. STOCKMANN.   Well, so you think——?

HOVSTAD.   You said yesterday that the water is polluted by impurities in the soil——

DR. STOCKMANN.   Yes, undoubtedly; the mischief comes from that poisonous swamp up in the Mill Dale.

HOVSTAD.   Excuse me, Doctor, but I think it comes from quite another swamp.

DR. STOCKMANN.   What swamp may that be?

HOVSTAD.   The swamp in which our whole municipal life is rotting.

DR. STOCKMANN.   The devil, Mr. Hovstad!   What notion is this you've got hold of?

HOVSTAD.   All the affairs of the town have gradually drifted into the hands of a pack of bureaucrats.

DR. STOCKMANN.   Come now, they're not all bureaucrats.

HOVSTAD.   No; but those who aren't are the friends and adherents of those who are.   We're entirely governed by a ring of wealthy men, men of old family and position in the town.

DR. STOCKMANN.   Yes, but they're also men of ability and insight.

HOVSTAD.   Did they show ability and insight when they laid the water-pipes where they are?

DR. STOCKMANN.   No; that was a piece of stupidity, of course.   But that'll be set right now.

HOVSTAD.   Do you think it'll go so smoothly?

DR. STOCKMANN.   Well, smoothly or not, it'll have to be done.

HOVSTAD. Yes, if the press exerts its influence.

DR. STOCKMANN. Not at all necessary, my dear fellow; I'm sure my brother——

HOVSTAD. Excuse me, Doctor, but I must tell you that I think of taking the matter up.

DR. STOCKMANN. In the paper?

HOVSTAD. Yes. When I took over the *People's Messenger*, I was determined to break up this ring of obstinate old blockheads who hold everything in their hands.

DR. STOCKMANN. But you told me yourself what came of it. You nearly ruined the paper.

HOVSTAD. Yes, we had to draw in our horns then, that's true enough. The whole Bath scheme might have fallen through if these men had been sent about their business. But now the Baths are an accomplished fact, and we can get on without these august personages.

DR. STOCKMANN. Get on without them, yes; but still we owe them much.

HOVSTAD. The debt shall be amply acknowledged. But a journalist of my democratic tendencies can't let such an opportunity slip through his fingers. We must explode the tradition of official infallibility. That rubbish must be got rid of, like every other superstition.

DR. STOCKMANN. I'm with you with all my heart, Mr. Hovstad. If it's a superstition, away with it.

HOVSTAD. I should be sorry to attack the Burgomaster, as he's your brother. But I know you think with me—the truth before all other considerations.

DR. STOCKMANN. Why, of course. (*Vehemently.*) But then—! but then——!

HOVSTAD. You mustn't think ill of me. I'm neither more self-interested nor more ambitious than other men.

DR. STOCKMANN. Why, my dear fellow, who says you are?

HOVSTAD. I come of humble folk, as you know, and I've had occasion to see what the lower classes really require. And that is to have a share in the direction of public affairs, Doctor. That's what develops ability and knowledge and self-respect——

DR. STOCKMANN. I understand that perfectly.

HOVSTAD. Yes; and I think a journalist incurs a heavy responsibility when he neglects an opportunity of helping to emancipate the downtrodden masses. I know well enough that our oligarchy will denounce me as an agitator, and so forth; but what do I care? If only my conscience is clear, I——

DR. STOCKMANN. Just so, just so, my dear Mr. Hovstad. But still—deuce take it——! (*A knock at the door.*) Come in!

    (ASLAKSEN, *the printer, appears at the door of the anteroom. He is humbly but neatly dressed in black, wearing a white necktie slightly crumpled, and carrying gloves and a silk hat.*)

ASLAKSEN (*bowing*). I beg pardon, Doctor, for making so bold——

DR. STOCKMANN (*rising*). Hallo! If it isn't Mr. Aslaksen!

ASLAKSEN. Yes, it's me, Doctor.

HOVSTAD (*rising*). Do you want me, Aslaksen?

ASLAKSEN. No, not at all. I didn't know you were here. No, it's the Doctor himself——

DR. STOCKMANN. Well, what can I do for you?

ASLAKSEN. Is it true what Mr. Billing says, that you're going to get us a better set of water-works?

DR. STOCKMANN. Yes, for the Baths.

ASLAKSEN. Of course, of course. Then I just looked in to say that I'll back up the movement with all my might.

HOVSTAD (*to the* DOCTOR). You see!

DR. STOCKMANN. I'm sure I thank you heartily; but——

ASLAKSEN. It'll do you no harm to have us middle-class men at your back. We now form what you may call a compact majority in the town—when we want to, that's to say. And it's always well to have the majority with you, Doctor.

DR. STOCKMANN. No doubt, no doubt; but I can't conceive that any special measures will be necessary. I should think in so clear and straightforward a matter——

ASLAKSEN. Yes, but all the same, it can do no harm; I know the local authorities well. The powers that be are not over ready to adopt suggestions from outsiders. So I think it wouldn't be amiss if we made some sort of a demonstration.

HOVSTAD. I think so too.

DR. STOCKMANN. A demonstration, you say? But how do you mean to demonstrate?

ASLAKSEN. Of course with great moderation, Doctor. I'm always in favour of moderation; for

moderation is a citizen's first virtue—at least that's
my way of thinking.

DR. STOCKMANN. We all know that, Mr.
Aslaksen.

ASLAKSEN. Yes, I think my moderation is generally recognised. And this affair of the water-works is
very important for us small middle-class men. The
Baths bid fair to become a little gold-mine for the
town. We'll all have to live by the Baths, especially
we householders. We want to support the Baths all
we can ; and as I'm Chairman of the Householders'
Association——

DR. STOCKMANN. Well——?

ASLAKSEN. And as I'm an active worker for the
Temperance[1] Society—of course you know, Doctor,
that I'm a temperance man ?

DR. STOCKMANN. To be sure, to be sure.

ASLAKSEN. Well, you'll understand that I come
in contact with a great many people. And as I'm
known to be a prudent and law-abiding citizen, as
you yourself admitted, Doctor, I have a certain
influence in the town, and hold some power in my
hands—though I say it that shouldn't.

DR. STOCKMANN. I know that very well, Mr.
Aslaksen.

ASLAKSEN. Well you see, it would be easy for me
to get up an address, if it came to a pinch.

DR. STOCKMANN. An address ?

ASLAKSEN. Yes, a kind of vote of thanks to you,
from the citizens of the town, for your action in a

[1] The word "mådehold," in Norwegian, means both "moderation"
and "temperance."

matter of such general concern. Of course it will have to be drawn up with befitting moderation, so as to give no offence to the authorities and persons of position. But so long as we're careful about that, no one can take it ill, I should think.

HOVSTAD. Well, even if they didn't particularly like it——

ASLAKSEN. No no no ; no offence to the powers that be, Mr. Hovstad. No opposition to people that can take it out of us again so easily. I've had enough of that in my time ; no good ever comes of it. But no one can object to the free but temperate expression of a citizen's opinion.

DR. STOCKMANN (*shaking his hand*). I can't tell you, my dear Mr. Aslaksen, how heartily it delights me to find so much support among my fellow-townsmen. I'm so happy—so happy! Come, you'll have a glass of sherry ? Eh ?

ASLAKSEN. No, thank you ; I never take wine.

DR. STOCKMANN. Well, then, a glass of beer— what do you say to that ?

ASLAKSEN. Thanks, not that either, Doctor. I never take anything so early in the day. And now I'll be off round the town, and talk to some of the householders, and prepare public opinion.

DR. STOCKMANN. It's extremely kind of you, Mr. Aslaksen ; but I really can't get it into my head that all these preparations are necessary ; it seems to me the affair's as simple as possible.

ASLAKSEN. The authorities always move slowly, Doctor— God forbid I should blame them for it——

HOVSTAD. We'll stir them up in the paper to-morrow, Aslaksen.

ASLAKSEN. No violence, Mr. Hovstad. Proceed with moderation, or you'll do nothing with them. Take my advice; I've picked up experience in the school of life. And now I'll say good-morning, Doctor. You know now that at least you have us small middle-class men behind you, solid as a wall. You have the compact majority on your side, Doctor!

DR. STOCKMANN. Many thanks, my dear Mr. Aslaksen. (*Holds out his hand.*) Good-bye, good-bye.

ASLAKSEN. Are you coming to the office, Mr. Hovstad?

HOVSTAD. I'll come on presently. I've something to settle first.

ASLAKSEN. All right.

(*Bows, and goes.* DR. STOCKMANN *accompanies him into the anteroom.*)

HOVSTAD (*as the* DOCTOR *re-enters*). Well, what do you say to that, Doctor? Don't you think it's high time we should strike a blow at all this weak-kneed trimming and cowardice?

DR. STOCKMANN. Are you speaking of Aslaksen?

HOVSTAD. Yes, I am. He's a decent enough fellow, but he's one of those who are sunk in the swamp. And most people here are just like him; they're for ever see-sawing from side to side; what with scruples and misgivings, they never dare advance a step.

DR. STOCKMANN. Yes, but Aslaksen seems to me thoroughly well-intentioned.

HOVSTAD.   There's one thing I value more highly than good intentions; and that is an attitude of manly self-reliance.

DR. STOCKMANN.   There I'm quite with you.

HOVSTAD.   So I'm going to seize this opportunity, and see whether I can't for once put a little grit into their good intentions.   The worship of authority must be rooted up in this town.   This gross, inexcusable blunder of the water-works should be enough to open the eyes of every voter.

DR. STOCKMANN.   Very well!   If you think it's for the good of the community, so be it; but not till I've spoken to my brother.

HOVSTAD.   Anyhow, I'll be writing my leader in the meantime.   And if the Burgomaster won't take the matter up——

DR. STOCKMANN.   But how can you conceive his refusing?

HOVSTAD.   Oh, it's not inconceivable.   And then——?

DR. STOCKMANN.   Well then, I promise you——; look here—then you may print my paper—put it in just as it is.

HOVSTAD.   May I?   Is that a promise?

DR. STOCKMANN (*handing him the manuscript*). There it is; take it with you.   You may as well read it in any case; you can return it to me afterwards.

HOVSTAD.   Very good; I'll do so.   And now, good-bye, Doctor.

DR. STOCKMANN.   Good-bye, good-bye.   You'll see it'll all go smoothly, Mr Hovstad—as smoothly as possible.

HOVSTAD. Hm! We shall see.

(*Bows and goes out through the anteroom.*)

DR. STOCKMANN (*going to the dining-room door and looking in*). Katrine! Hallo! you back, Petra?

PETRA (*entering*). Yes, I've just got back from school.

MRS. STOCKMANN (*entering*). Hasn't he been here yet?

DR. STOCKMANN. Peter? No; but I've been having a long talk with Hovstad. He's quite enthusiastic about my discovery. You see, it's of much wider import than I thought at first. So he's placed his paper at my disposal, if I should require it.

MRS. STOCKMANN. Do you think you will——?

DR. STOCKMANN. Not I! But all the same, one's proud to know that the enlightened, independent press is on one's side. And what do you think? I've had a visit from the Chairman of the Householders' Association too.

MRS. STOCKMANN. Really! What did he want?

DR. STOCKMANN. To assure me of his support. They'll stand by me at a pinch. Katrine, do you know what I have behind me?

MRS. STOCKMANN. Behind you? No. What have you behind you?

DR. STOCKMANN. The compact majority!

MRS. STOCKMANN. Oh! Is that good for you, Thomas?

DR. STOCKMANN. Yes, indeed; I should think it was good! (*Rubbing his hands as he walks up and down.*) Great God! what a delight it is to feel oneself in such brotherly concord with one's fellow-townsmen.

PETRA. And to do so much that's good and useful, father!

DR. STOCKMANN. And all for one's native town, too!

MRS. STOCKMANN. There's the bell.

DR. STOCKMANN. That must be he. (*Knock at the door.*) Come in!

(*Enter* BURGOMASTER STOCKMANN *from the anteroom.*)

BURGOMASTER. Good-morning.

DR. STOCKMANN. I'm glad to see you, Peter.

MRS. STOCKMANN. Good-morning, brother-in-law. How are you?

BURGOMASTER. Oh, thanks, so-so. (*To the* DOCTOR.) Yesterday evening, after office hours, I received from you a dissertation upon the water at the Baths.

DR. STOCKMANN. Yes. Have you read it?

BURGOMASTER. I have.

DR. STOCKMANN. And what do you think of the affair?

BURGOMASTER. Hm—— (*Glancing at the women.*)

MRS. STOCKMANN. Come, Petra.

(*She and* PETRA *go into the room, left.*)

BURGOMASTER (*after a pause*). Was it necessary to make all these investigations behind my back?

DR. STOCKMANN. Yes, till I was absolutely certain, I——

BURGOMASTER. So you're certain now?

DR. STOCKMANN. You found no uncertainty in my statement of the case, did you?

BURGOMASTER. Is it your intention to submit

this statement to the Board of Directors, as a sort of official document?

DR. STOCKMANN. Of course. Something must be done in the matter, and that promptly.

BURGOMASTER. As usual, you use very strong expressions in your statement. Amongst other things, you say that what we offer our visitors is a slow poison!

DR. STOCKMANN. Why, Peter, can you call it anything else? Only think—poisoned water both internally and externally! And that to poor invalids who come to us in all confidence, and pay us liberally to cure them!

BURGOMASTER. And then you announce as your conclusion that we must build a sewer to carry off all the alleged impurities from the Mill Dale, and relay all the water-pipes.

DR. STOCKMANN. Yes. Can you suggest any alternative?—I know of none.

BURGOMASTER. I made an excuse for looking in at the town engineer's this morning, and—in a half-jesting way—I mentioned these alterations as things we might possibly have to consider, at some future time.

DR. STOCKMANN. At some future time!

BURGOMASTER. Of course he smiled at what he thought my extravagance. Have you taken the trouble to think what your proposed alterations would cost? From what the engineer said, I gathered that the expenses would probably mount up to several hundred thousand crowns.

DR. STOCKMANN. So much as that?

BURGOMASTER. Yes. But that's not the worst. The work would take at least two years.

DR. STOCKMANN. Two years! Do you mean to say two whole years?

BURGOMASTER. At least. And what are we to do with the Baths in the meanwhile? Are we to close them? Of course we'd have to. Do you think any one would come here, if it got abroad that the water was pestilential?

DR. STOCKMANN. But, Peter, that's just what it is.

BURGOMASTER. And all this now, just now, when the Baths are doing so well! Neighbouring towns, too, are not without their claims to rank as health-resorts. Do you think they wouldn't at once set to work to divert the full stream of visitors to themselves? Undoubtedly they would; and we should be left stranded. We should probably have to give up the whole costly undertaking; and so you would have ruined your native town.

DR. STOCKMANN. I—ruined——!

BURGOMASTER. It's only through the Baths that the town has any future worth speaking of. You surely know that as well as I do.

DR. STOCKMANN. But what do you think should be done?

BURGOMASTER. I have not succeeded in convincing myself that the condition of the water at the Baths is as serious as your statement represents.

DR. STOCKMANN. I tell you it's if anything worse —or will be in the summer, when the hot weather sets in.

BURGOMASTER. I repeat that I believe you exaggerate greatly. A competent physician should know what measures to take in order to obviate injurious influences, and to counteract them in case they should make themselves unmistakably felt.

DR. STOCKMANN. Indeed——? And then——?

BURGOMASTER. The existing water-works are, after all, a fact, and must naturally be treated as such. But when the time comes, the Directors will probably not be indisposed to consider whether it may not be possible, without unreasonable pecuniary sacrifices, to introduce certain improvements.

DR. STOCKMANN. And do you imagine I could ever be a party to such dishonesty?

BURGOMASTER. Dishonesty?

DR. STOCKMANN. Yes, it would be dishonesty— a fraud, a lie, an absolute crime against the public, against society as a whole!

BURGOMASTER. I have not, as I before remarked, been able to convince myself that there is really any such imminent danger.

DR. STOCKMANN. You have—you must have! I'm sure my demonstration is absolutely clear and convincing. And you know that perfectly, Peter, only you won't admit it. It was you who insisted that both the Bath-buildings and the water-works should be placed where they now are ; and it's *that*— it's that damned blunder that you won't confess. Pshaw ! Do you think I don't see through you ?

BURGOMASTER. And even if it were so? If I do watch over my reputation with a certain anxiety, I do it for the good of the town. Without moral authority

I cannot guide and direct affairs in the way I consider most conducive to the general welfare. Therefore—and on various other grounds—it is of great moment to me that your statement should not be submitted to the Board of Directors. It must be kept back, for the good of the community. Later on I will bring up the matter for discussion, and we'll do the best we can, quietly; but not a word, not a whisper, of this unfortunate business must come to the public ears.

DR. STOCKMANN. But it can't be prevented now, my dear Peter.

BURGOMASTER. It must and shall be prevented.

DR. STOCKMANN. It can't be, I tell you; far too many people know about it already.

BURGOMASTER. Know about it! Who? Surely not those fellows on the *People's Messenger*——?

DR. STOCKMANN. Oh yes; they know. The liberal, independent press will take good care you do your duty.

BURGOMASTER (*after a short pause*). You're an amazingly reckless man, Thomas. Haven't you reflected what the consequences of this may be to yourself?

DR. STOCKMANN. Consequences?—Consequences to me?

BURGOMASTER. Yes—to you and yours.

DR. STOCKMANN. What the devil do you mean?

BURGOMASTER. I believe I've always shown myself ready and willing to lend you a helping hand.

DR. STOCKMANN. Yes, you have, and I thank you for it.

BURGOMASTER. I ask for no thanks. I was in

some measure forced to act as I did—for my own sake. I always hoped I should be able to keep you within certain bounds, if I helped to improve your pecuniary position.

DR. STOCKMANN. What! So it was only for your own sake—— !

BURGOMASTER. In a measure, I say. It is painful for a man in an official position, when his nearest relation goes and compromises himself time after time.

DR. STOCKMANN. And you think I do that?

BURGOMASTER. Yes, unfortunately, you do, without knowing it. Yours is a turbulent, pugnacious, rebellious spirit. And then you have an unhappy propensity for rushing into print upon every possible and impossible occasion. You no sooner hit upon an idea than you must needs write a newspaper article or a whole pamphlet about it.

DR. STOCKMANN. Isn't it a citizen's duty, when he has conceived a new idea, to communicate it to the public!

BURGOMASTER. Pshaw! The public doesn't need new ideas. The public gets on best with the good old recognised ideas it has already.

DR. STOCKMANN. You say that right out!

BURGOMASTER. Yes, I must speak frankly to you for once. Hitherto I've tried to avoid it, for I know how irritable you are; but now I'm bound to tell you the truth, Thomas. You've no conception how much you injure yourself by your rashness. You complain of the authorities, ay, of the Government itself—you cry them down and maintain you've been slighted, persecuted. But what else can you expect, with your impossible disposition.

DR. STOCKMANN.   Oh, indeed ! So I'm impossible, am I ?

BURGOMASTER.   Yes, Thomas, you're an impossible man to work with.   I know that from experience.   You have no consideration ; you seem quite to forget that you have me to thank for your position as medical officer of the Baths——

DR. STOCKMANN.   It was mine by right !   Mine, and no one else's !   I was the first to discover the town's capabilities as a watering-place ; I saw them, and, at that time, I alone.   For years I fought single-handed for this idea of mine ; I wrote and wrote——

BURGOMASTER.   No doubt ; but then the right time hadn't come.   Of course in that out-of-the-world corner you couldn't judge of that.   As soon as the propitious moment came, I—and others—took the matter in hand——

DR. STOCKMANN.   Yes, and you bungled the whole of my glorious plan.   Oh, we see now what a set of wiseacres you were!

BURGOMASTER.   All *I* can see is that you're again seeking an outlet for your pugnacity.   You want to make an onslaught on your superiors —that's an old habit of yours.   You can't endure any authority over you ; you look askance at any one who has a higher post than your own ; you regard him as a personal enemy—and then it's all one to you what kind of weapon you use against him. But now I've shown you how much is at stake for the town, and consequently for me too.   And therefore

I warn you, Thomas, that I'm inexorable in the demand I am about to make of you!

DR. STOCKMANN. What demand?

BURGOMASTER. As you haven't had the sense to refrain from chattering to outsiders about this delicate business, which should have been kept an official secret, of course it can't now be hushed up. All sorts of rumours will get abroad, and evil-disposed persons will invent all sorts of additions to them. It will therefore be necessary for you publicly to contradict these rumours.

DR. STOCKMANN. I? How? I don't understand you.

BURGOMASTER. We expect that after further investigation you will come to the conclusion that the affair is not nearly so serious or pressing as you had at first imagined.

DR. STOCKMANN. Aha! So you expect that?

BURGOMASTER. Furthermore, we expect you to express your confidence that the Board of Directors will thoroughly and conscientiously carry out all measures for the removal of any possible drawback.

DR. STOCKMANN. Yes, but you'll never be able to do that, so long as you go on tinkering and patching. I tell you that, Peter; and it's my deepest, sincerest conviction——

BURGOMASTER. As an official, you have no right to have any individual conviction.

DR. STOCKMANN (*starting*). No right to any——?

BURGOMASTER. As an official, I say. In your private capacity, of course, it's another matter. But as a subordinate official of the Baths, you've no right to express any conviction at issue with that of your superiors.

DR. STOCKMANN. This is too much! I, a doctor, a man of science, have no right to——

BURGOMASTER. The matter in question is not a purely scientific one; it's a complex affair; it has both a technical and an economic side.

DR. STOCKMANN. Pshaw! What's that to me? What the devil do I care! I will be free to speak my mind upon any subject on earth!

BURGOMASTER. As you please—so long as it doesn't concern the Baths. With them we forbid you to meddle.

DR. STOCKMANN (*shouts*). You forbid——! you! —a set of——

BURGOMASTER. *I* forbid it—*I*, your chief; and you must obey my prohibition.

DR. STOCKMANN (*controlling himself*). Upon my word, Peter, if you weren't my brother——

PETRA (*tears open the door*). Father, you shan't submit to this!

MRS. STOCKMANN (*following her*). Petra, Petra!

BURGOMASTER. Ah! so we've been listening!

MRS. STOCKMANN. The partition's so thin, we couldn't help——

PETRA. I stood and listened on purpose.

BURGOMASTER. Well, on the whole, I'm not sorry——

DR. STOCKMANN (*coming nearer to him*). You spoke to me of forbidding and obeying——

BURGOMASTER. You forced me to adopt that tone.

DR. STOCKMANN. And I am to give myself the lie, in a public declaration ?

BURGOMASTER. We consider it absolutely necessary that you should issue a statement in the terms indicated.

DR. STOCKMANN. And if I don't obey ?

BURGOMASTER. Then we shall ourselves put forth a statement to reassure the public.

DR. STOCKMANN. Well and good ; then I'll write against you. I shall stick to my point and prove that *I* am right, and you wrong. And what will you do then ?

BURGOMASTER. Then I shall be unable to prevent your dismissal.

DR. STOCKMANN. What——!

PETRA. Father ! Dismissal !

MRS. STOCKMANN. Dismissal !

BURGOMASTER. Your dismissal from the Baths. I shall be obliged to move that notice be given you at once, and that you have henceforth no connection whatever with the Baths.

DR. STOCKMANN. You would dare to do that !

BURGOMASTER. It is you who are playing the daring game.

PETRA. Uncle, this is scandalous conduct towards a man like father.

MRS. STOCKMANN. Do be quiet, Petra.

BURGOMASTER (*looking at* PETRA). Aha ! We have opinions of our own already, eh ? Of course ! (*To* MRS. STOCKMANN.) Sister-in-law, you are apparently the most sensible person in the house. Use all your influence with your husband ; try to make him realise what all this will involve both for his family——

DR. STOCKMANN. My family concerns myself alone.

BURGOMASTER. ——Both for his family, I say, and for the town he lives in.

DR. STOCKMANN. It's I that have the real good of the town at heart! I want to lay bare the evils that, sooner or later, must come to light. Ah! You shall yet see that I love my native town.

BURGOMASTER. You, who, in your blind obstinacy, want to cut off the town's chief source of prosperity!

DR. STOCKMANN. The source is poisoned, man! Are you mad? We live by trafficking in filth and corruption. The whole of our flourishing social life is rooted in a lie!

BURGOMASTER. Idle fancies—or worse. The man who makes such offensive insinuations against his native place must be an enemy of society.

DR. STOCKMANN (*going towards him*). You dare to——

MRS. STOCKMANN (*throwing herself between them*). Thomas!

PETRA (*seizing her father's arm*). Keep calm, father.

BURGOMASTER. I won't expose myself to violence. You're warned now. Reflect upon what is due to yourself and to your family. Good-bye.

(*He goes.*)

DR. STOCKMANN (*walking up and down*). And I must put up with such treatment! In my own house, Katrine! What do you say to that?

MRS. STOCKMANN.   Indeed it's a shame and a disgrace, Thomas——

PETRA.   Oh, I'd like to give it to uncle——!

DR. STOCKMANN.   It's my own fault.   I ought to have bristled up against them long ago—to have shown my teeth—and made them feel them!   And he called me an enemy of society.   Me!   I won't bear it; by Heaven, I won't!

MRS. STOCKMANN.   But, my dear Thomas, after all, your brother has the power——

DR. STOCKMANN.   Yes, but I have the right!

MRS. STOCKMANN.   Ah yes, right, right!   What's the good of having the right when you haven't the might?

PETRA.   Oh mother! how can you talk so?

DR. STOCKMANN.   What!   No good, in a free society, to have right on your side?   I like that, Katrine!   And besides, haven't I the free and independent press with me, and the compact majority at my back?   That's might enough, I should think!

MRS. STOCKMANN.   Why, good heavens, Thomas! you're surely not thinking of——?

DR. STOCKMANN.   What am I not thinking of?

MRS. STOCKMANN.   Of setting yourself up against your brother, I mean.

DR. STOCKMANN.   What the devil would you have me do, if not stick to what's right and true?

PETRA.   Yes, that's what I'd like to know?

MRS. STOCKMANN.   But it'll be of no earthly use. If they won't they won't.

DR. STOCKMANN.   Ho-ho, Katrine! just wait a while and you'll see I can fight my own battles.

MRS. STOCKMANN. Yes, you'll fight—till you get your dismissal; that's what'll happen.

DR. STOCKMANN. Well then, I shall at any rate have done my duty towards the public, towards society—I who am called an enemy of society!

MRS. STOCKMANN. But towards your family, Thomas? Towards us at home? Do you think this is doing your duty towards those who are dependent on you?

PETRA. Oh mother, don't always think first of us.

MRS. STOCKMANN. Yes, it's all very well for you to talk; you can stand alone if need be.—But think of the boys, Thomas; and think a little of yourself too, and of me——

DR. STOCKMANN. You're surely out of your senses, Katrine. Am I to be such a miserable coward as to knuckle under to this Peter and his damned crew? Should I ever have another happy hour in all my life?

MRS. STOCKMANN. I don't know; but God preserve us from the happiness we shall all of us have if you stick to your point. There you would be again, with nothing to live on, with no regular income. I think we had enough of that in the old days. Remember them, Thomas; think of what it all means.

DR. STOCKMANN (*struggling with himself and clenching his hands*). And these jacks-in-office can bring all this upon a free and honest man! Isn't it disgusting, Katrine?

MRS. STOCKMANN. Yes, no doubt they're treating

you shamefully. But God knows there's plenty of injustice one must just submit to in this world.— Here are the boys, Thomas. Look at them! What's to become of them? Oh no, no! you can never have the heart——

(EILIF *and* MORTEN, *with school-books, have meanwhile entered.*)

DR. STOCKMANN. The boys——! (*With a sudden access of firmness and decision.*) Never, though the whole earth should crumble, will I bow my neck beneath the yoke.

(*Goes towards his room.*)

MRS. STOCKMANN (*following him*). Thomas, what are you going to do?

DR. STOCKMANN (*at the door*). I must have the right to look my boys in the face when they've grown into free men.

(*Goes into his room.*)

MRS. STOCKMANN (*bursts into tears*). Ah! God help us all!

PETRA. Father's all right! He'll never give in!

(*The boys ask wonderingly what it all means; PETRA signs to them to be quiet.*)

Act Third.

(The Editor's Room; office of the "People's Messenger." In the background, to the left, a door; to the right another door, with glass panes, through which can be seen the printing-room. A door in the right-hand wall. In the middle of the room a large table covered with papers, newspapers, and books. In front, on the left, a window, and by it a writing-desk with a high stool. A couple of arm-chairs beside the table; some other chairs along the walls. The room is dingy and cheerless, the furniture shabby, the arm-chairs dirty and torn. Within the printing-room are seen a few compositors at work; further within, a hand-press in operation.)

(HOVSTAD is seated at the desk, writing. Presently BILLING enters from the right, with the DOCTOR'S manuscript in his hand.)

BILLING. Well, I must say——

HOVSTAD *(writing)*. Have you read it through?

BILLING *(laying MS. on the desk)*. Yes, I should think I had.

HOVSTAD. Don't you think the Doctor comes out strong——?

BILLING. Strong! Why, strike me dead if he isn't crushing! Every word falls like a—well, like a sledge-hammer.

HOVSTAD. Yes, but these fellows won't collapse at the first blow.

BILLING. True enough; but we'll keep on hammering away, blow after blow, till the whole bureaucracy comes crashing down. As I sat in there reading that article, I seemed to hear the revolution thundering afar.

HOVSTAD (*turning round*). Hush! Don't let Aslaksen hear that.

BILLING (*in a lower voice*). Aslaksen's a white-livered, cowardly fellow, without a spark of manhood in him. But this time surely you'll have your own way? You'll print the Doctor's paper?

HOVSTAD. Yes, if only the Burgomaster doesn't give in——

BILLING. That would be deuced annoying.

HOVSTAD. Well, whatever happens, fortunately we can turn the situation to account. If the Burgomaster won't agree to the Doctor's proposal, he'll have all the small middle-class against him—all the Householders' Association, and the rest of them. And if he does agree to it, he'll fall out with the whole crew of big shareholders in the Baths, who have hitherto been his main support——

BILLING. Yes, of course; for it's certain they'll have to fork out a lot of money——

HOVSTAD. You may take your oath of that. And then, don't you see, when the ring is broken up, we'll din it into the public day by day that the Burgomaster is incompetent in every respect, and that all positions of trust in the town, the whole municipal government in short, must be entrusted to men of liberal ideas.

BILLING. Strike me dead if that isn't the square

truth. I see it, I see it: we're on the eve of a revolution!

(*A knock at the door.*)

HOVSTAD. Hush—(*calls*). Come in!

(DR. STOCKMANN *enters from the back, left.*)

HOVSTAD (*going towards him*). Ah! here's the Doctor. Well?

DR. STOCKMANN. Print away, Mr. Hovstad!

HOVSTAD. So it's come to that?

BILLING. Hurrah!

DR. STOCKMANN. Print away, I tell you. To be sure it's come to that. Since they will have it so, they must! War is declared, Mr. Billing!

BILLING. War to the knife, say I! War to the death, Doctor!

DR. STOCKMANN. This article is only the beginning. I've got plans for four or five others in my head already. But where do you keep Aslaksen?

BILLING (*calling into the printing-room*). Aslaksen! just come here a moment.

HOVSTAD. Did you say four or five more articles? On the same subject?

DR. STOCKMANN. Not at all, my dear fellow. No; they'll deal with quite different matters. But they're all of a piece with the water-works and sewer question. One thing leads to another. It's like beginning to pick at an old house, don't you know?

BILLING. Strike me dead, but that's true! You feel you can't leave off till you've pulled the whole rubbish to pieces.

ASLAKSEN (*enters from the printing-room*). Pulled

to pieces! Surely the Doctor isn't thinking of pulling the Baths to pieces?

HOVSTAD. Not at all! Don't be alarmed.

DR. STOCKMANN. No, we were talking of something quite different. Well, what do you think of my article, Mr. Hovstad?

HOVSTAD. I think it's simply a masterpiece——

DR. STOCKMANN. Yes, isn't it? I'm glad you think so—so glad.

HOVSTAD. It's so clear and to the point. One doesn't in the least need to be a specialist to understand the gist of it. I'm sure every intelligent man will be on your side.

ASLAKSEN. And all the prudent ones too, I hope?

BILLING. Both the prudent and imprudent—in fact, almost the whole town.

ASLAKSEN. Then I suppose we may venture to print it.

DR. STOCKMANN. I should think so!

HOVSTAD. It shall go in to-morrow.

DR. STOCKMANN. Yes, plague take it, not a day must be lost. Look here, Mr. Aslaksen, this is what I wanted to ask you: won't you take personal charge of the article?

ASLAKSEN. Certainly I will.

DR. STOCKMANN. Be as careful as if it were gold. No printers' errors; every word is important. I'll look in again presently; perhaps you'll be able to let me see a proof. Ah! I can't tell you how I long to have the thing in print—to see it hurled forth——

BILLING. Yes, like a thunderbolt!

DR. STOCKMANN. ——and submitted to the

judgment of every intelligent citizen. Oh! you've no idea what I've had to put up with to-day. I've been threatened with all sorts of things. I was to be robbed of my clearest rights as a man——

BILLING. What! Your rights as a man——!

DR. STOCKMANN. ——I was to humble myself, and eat the dust; I was to set my personal interests above my deepest, holiest convictions——

BILLING. Strike me dead, but that's too outrageous!

HOVSTAD. Oh, what can you expect from that quarter?

DR. STOCKMANN. But they'll get the worst of it, I can promise them. I'll throw myself into the breach every day in the *Messenger*, bombard them with one explosive article after another——

ASLAKSEN. Yes, but look here——

BILLING. Hurrah! War! War!

DR. STOCKMANN. I'll smite them to the earth, I'll crush them, I'll level their entrenchments to the ground in the eyes of all right-thinking men! I'll do it!

ASLAKSEN. But above all things be temperate, Doctor; proceed with moderation——

BILLING. Not at all, not at all! don't spare the dynamite!

DR. STOCKMANN (*going on imperturbably*). For now it isn't merely a question of water-works and sewers, you see. No, society as a whole must be purged, disinfected——

BILLING. There sounded the word of salvation!

DR. STOCKMANN. All the old bunglers must be

got rid of, you understand. And that in every depart-
ment! Such endless vistas have opened out before
me to-day. I don't see everything quite clearly yet,
but that'll soon come. It's young and vigorous
standard-bearers we must look for, my friends; we
must have new captains at all the outposts.

BILLING. Hear, hear!

DR. STOCKMANN. And if only we hold together,
it'll go so smoothly, so smoothly! The whole revolution will be just like the launch of a ship. Don't you
think so?

HOVSTAD. For my part, I believe we have now
every prospect of placing our municipal affairs in the
right hands.

ASLAKSEN. And if only we proceed with
moderation, I really don't think there can be any
danger.

DR. STOCKMANN. Who the devil cares whether
there's danger or not? What I do, I do in the name
of truth and for conscience sake.

HOVSTAD. You are a man to be backed up,
Doctor.

ASLAKSEN. Yes, there's no doubt the Doctor's a
true friend to the town; he's what I call a friend of
society.

BILLING. Strike me dead if Dr. Stockmann isn't
a Friend of the People, Aslaksen.

ASLAKSEN. I have no doubt the Householders'
Association will soon adopt that expression.

DR. STOCKMANN (*shaking their hands, deeply moved*).
Thanks, thanks, my dear, faithful friends; it does me
good to hear you. My respected brother called me

something very different. Never mind! I'll pay him back with interest! But I must be off now to see a poor devil of a patient. I'll look in again, though. Be sure you look after the article, Mr. Aslaksen; and for goodness' sake don't leave out any of my notes of exclamation! Rather put in a few more. Well, good-bye for the present, good-bye, good-bye.

(*Mutual salutations while they accompany him to the door. He goes out.*)

HOVSTAD. He'll be invaluable to us.

ASLAKSEN. Yes, so long as he confines himself to the Baths. But if he goes further, it won't be advisable to go with him.

HOVSTAD. Hm! Well, that depends——

BILLING. You're always so confoundedly timid, Aslaksen.

ASLAKSEN. Timid? Yes, when it's a question of attacking local authorities, I *am* timid, Mr. Billing; I have learnt caution in the school of experience, let me tell you. But go for the higher politics, attack the Government itself, and then see if I'm timid.

BILLING. No, you're not; but that's just where you're inconsistent.

ASLAKSEN. The fact is, I'm keenly alive to my responsibilities. If you attack the Government, you at least do society no harm, for the men attacked don't care a straw, you see; they stay where they are all the same. But *local* authorities *can* be turned out; and then we might get some incompetent set into power, to the irreparable injury both of householders and others.

HOVSTAD. But the education of citizens by self-government—what do you think of *that*?

ASLAKSEN. When a man has solid interests to protect, he can't think of everything, Mr. Hovstad.

HOVSTAD. Then I hope I may never have solid interests to protect.

BILLING. Hear, hear!

ASLAKSEN (*smiling*). Hm! (*Points to the desk.*) Governor Stensgård[1] sat in that editorial chair before you.

BILLING (*spitting*). Pooh! A turncoat like that!

HOVSTAD. I'm no weathercock—and never will be.

ASLAKSEN. A politician should never be too sure of anything on earth, Mr. Hovstad. And as for you, Mr. Billing, you ought to take in a reef or two, I should say; aren't you applying for the secretaryship to the Town Council?

BILLING. I——!

HOVSTAD. Is that so, Billing?

BILLING. Well, yes—but, deuce take it, you know, I'm only doing it to annoy those wiseacres.

ASLAKSEN. Well, that doesn't concern me. But if I'm to be accused of cowardice and inconsistency, I'd just like to point out this: My political record is open to every one. I've not changed at all, except that I'm perhaps more moderate. My heart still belongs to the people; but I don't deny that my reason

---

[1] This is the only case in which Ibsen introduces persons who have appeared in an earlier play. Aslaksen figures in *The League of Youth*, of which Stensgård is the central character. It should be noted that Stensgård has justified Lundestad's prophecy by attaining the high administrative dignity of "Stiftamtmand," here roughly translated "Governor."

inclines somewhat towards the authorities—the local ones, at any rate.

(*Goes into the printing-room.*)

BILLING. Don't you think we ought to get rid of him, Hovstad?

HOVSTAD. Do you know of any one else that'll back us up, financially?

BILLING. What a confounded nuisance it is to have no capital!

HOVSTAD (*sitting down by desk*). Yes, if we only had that——

BILLING. Suppose you applied to Dr. Stockmann?

HOVSTAD (*turning over his papers*). What would be the good? He hasn't a rap.

BILLING. No; but he has a good man behind him—old Morten Kiil—"The Badger," as they call him.

HOVSTAD (*writing*). Are you so sure he has money?

BILLING. Yes, strike me dead if he hasn't! And part of it must certainly go to Stockmann's family. He's bound to provide for them—anyhow, for the children.

HOVSTAD (*half turning*). Are you counting on *that*?

BILLING. Counting? How should I be counting on it?

HOVSTAD. Best not! And that secretaryship you shouldn't count on either; for I can assure you you won't get it.

BILLING. Do you think I don't know that? A refusal is the very thing I want. Such a rebuff fires your spirit of opposition, gives you a fresh supply of gall ; and that's just what you need in a god-forsaken place like this, where there's so little to stimulate you.

HOVSTAD (*writing*). Yes, yes.

BILLING. Well—they'll soon hear of me ! Now I'll go and write the appeal to the Householders' Association.

(*Goes into the room on the right.*)

HOVSTAD (*sits at his desk, gnawing his pen, and says slowly*). Hm !—so that's it—(*A knock at the door*). Come in. (PETRA *enters from the back, left.*)

HOVSTAD (*rising*). What ! Is it you ? Here ?

PETRA. Yes ; please excuse me——

HOVSTAD (*offering her an arm-chair*). Won't you sit down.

PETRA. No, thanks ; I must go again directly.

HOVSTAD. I suppose it's something from your father——?

PETRA. No, I've come on my own account. (*Takes a book from the pocket of her cloak.*) Here's that English story.

HOVSTAD. Why have you brought it back ?

PETRA. Because I won't translate it.

HOVSTAD. But you promised——

PETRA. Yes ; but then I hadn't read it. I suppose you've not read it either ?

HOVSTAD. No ; you know I can't read English; but——

PETRA. Exactly; and that's why I wanted to tell you that you must find something else. (*Putting book on table.*) This can't possibly go into the *Messenger.*

HOVSTAD. Why not?

PETRA. Because it flies in the face of all your convictions.

HOVSTAD. Well, for that matter——

PETRA. You don't understand me. It's all about a supernatural power that looks after the so-called good people in this world, and turns everything to their advantage at last; while all the bad people are punished.

HOVSTAD. Yes, but that's all right. It's the very thing the public like.

PETRA. And would you supply the public with such stuff? You don't believe a word of it yourself. You know well enough that things don't really happen like that.

HOVSTAD. Of course not; but an editor can't always do as he likes. He has often to yield to people's fancies in small matters. After all, politics is the chief thing in life—at any rate for a newspaper; and if I want the people to follow me along the path of emancipation and progress, I mustn't scare them away. If they find a moral story like this down in the cellar,[1] they're all the more willing to stand what's printed above it—they feel themselves safer.

PETRA. For shame! You're not such a hypocrite as to spread snares like that for your readers. You're not a spider.

HOVSTAD (*smiling*). Thanks for your good opinion. It's true that the idea is Billing's, not mine.

[1] The reference is to the continental feuilleton at the foot of the page.

PETRA. Billing's!

HOVSTAD. Yes, at least he was talking in that strain the other day. It was Billing that was so anxious to get the story into the paper; I don't even know the book.

PETRA. But how can Billing, with his advanced views——

HOVSTAD. Well, Billing is many-sided. He's applying for the secretaryship to the Town Council, I hear.

PETRA. I don't believe that, Hovstad. How could he descend to such a thing?

HOVSTAD. That you must ask *him*.

PETRA. I could never have thought it of Billing.

HOVSTAD (*looking more closely at her*). No? Is that such a revelation to you?

PETRA. Yes. And yet—perhaps not. Oh, I don't know.

HOVSTAD. We journalists aren't worth much, Miss Petra.

PETRA. Do you really say that?

HOVSTAD. I think so, now and then.

PETRA. Yes, in the little everyday squabbles— that I can understand. But now that you've taken up a great cause——

HOVSTAD. You mean this affair of your father's?

PETRA. Of course. I should think you must feel yourself worth more than the common herd now.

HOVSTAD. Yes, to-day I do feel something of the sort.

PETRA. Yes, surely you must. Oh, it's a glorious career you've chosen! To be the pioneer of unrecognised truths and new and courageous ways of thought !—to stand forth fearlessly in support of an injured man——

HOVSTAD. Especially when the injured man is—hm !—I hardly know how to put it——

PETRA. You mean when he is so upright and true ?

HOVSTAD (*in a low voice*). I mean when he's your father——

PETRA (*suddenly taken aback*). *That ?*

HOVSTAD. Yes, Petra—Miss Petra.

PETRA. So *that's* your main idea, is it ? Not the cause itself ? Not the truth ? Not father's great, warm heart ?

HOVSTAD. Oh, that too, of course.

PETRA. No thank you ; you've said too much, Mr. Hovstad. Now I shall never trust you again in anything.

HOVSTAD. Can you be so hard on me because it's chiefly for your sake—— ?

PETRA. What I blame you for is that you haven't acted straightforwardly towards father. You've spoken to him as if you cared only for the truth and the good of the community. You've trifled with both father and me. You are not the man you pretended to be. And that I shall never forgive you—never !

HOVSTAD. You shouldn't say that so bitterly, Miss Petra—least of all now.

PETRA. Why not now ?

HOVSTAD. Because your father can't do without my help.

PETRA (*looking scornfully at him*). So that's what you are! Oh, shame!

HOVSTAD. No, no. I spoke thoughtlessly. You mustn't believe that.

PETRA. I know what to believe. Good-bye.

(ASLAKSEN *enters from printing-room, hurriedly and mysteriously.*)

ASLAKSEN. Plague take it, Mr. Hovstad—(*seeing* PETRA). Ow, that's awkward——

PETRA. Well, there's the book. You must give it to some one else.

(*Going towards the main door.*)

HOVSTAD (*following her*). But, Miss Petra——

PETRA. Good-bye. (*She goes.*)

ASLAKSEN. I say, Mr. Hovstad!

HOVSTAD. Well well; what is it?

ASLAKSEN. The Burgomaster's out there, in the printing-office.

HOVSTAD. The Burgomaster?

ASLAKSEN. Yes. He wants to speak to you; he came in by the back way—he didn't want to be seen, you know.

HOVSTAD. What's the meaning of this? Stop, I'll go myself—— (*Goes towards the printing-room, opens the door, bows, and invites the* BURGO-MASTER *to enter.*) Keep a look-out, Aslaksen, that no one——

ASLAKSEN. I understand.

(*Goes into the printing-room.*)

BURGOMASTER. You didn't expect to see me here, Mr. Hovstad.

HOVSTAD. No, I can't say I did.

BURGOMASTER (*looking about him*). You've got a very comfortable place here ; quite charming.

HOVSTAD. Oh——

BURGOMASTER. And here have I come, without with your leave or by your leave, to take up your time——

HOVSTAD. You're very welcome, sir ; I'm at your service. Let me take your cap and stick. (*He does so, and puts them on a chair.*) And won't you sit down ?

BURGOMASTER (*sitting down by the table*). Thanks. (HOVSTAD *also sits by the table.*) I've been much— very much worried to-day, Mr. Hovstad.

HOVSTAD. Really? Well, I suppose with all your various duties, Burgomaster——

BURGOMASTER. It's the Doctor that's been worry-ing me to-day.

HOVSTAD. Indeed ! The Doctor ?

BURGOMASTER. He's been writing a sort of memorandum to the Directors about some supposed shortcomings in the Baths.

HOVSTAD. Has he really ?

BURGOMASTER. Yes ; hasn't he told you ? I thought he said——

HOVSTAD. Oh yes, by-the-bye, he did say some-thing——

ASLAKSEN (*from the printing-office*). Oh, I want the manuscrift——

HOVSTAD (*in a tone of vexation*). Hm ; there it is on the desk.

ASLAKSEN (*finding it*). All right.

BURGOMASTER. Why, that's it——

ASLAKSEN. Yes, that's the Doctor's article, Burgo-master.

HOVSTAD. Oh! is *that* what you were speaking of?

BURGOMASTER. The very same. What do you think of it?

HOVSTAD. I'm not a specialist, and I've only glanced at it.

BURGOMASTER. And yet you're going to print it?

HOVSTAD. I can't very well refuse a signed com-munication——

ASLAKSEN. I have nothing to do with the editing of the paper, Burgomaster——

BURGOMASTER. Of course not.

ASLAKSEN. I merely print what's placed in my hands.

BURGOMASTER. Quite right, quite right.

ASLAKSEN. So I must——

(Goes towards the printing-room.)

BURGOMASTER. No, stop a moment, Mr. Aslaksen. With your permission, Mr. Hovstad——

HOVSTAD. By all means, Burgomaster.

BURGOMASTER. You're a discreet and thoughtful man, Mr. Aslaksen.

ASLAKSEN. I'm glad you think so, Burgomaster.

BURGOMASTER. And a man of very wide influence.

ASLAKSEN. Chiefly among the lower middle-class.

BURGOMASTER. The small tax-payers form the majority—here as everywhere.

ASLAKSEN. That's true enough.

BURGOMASTER. And I don't doubt that you know the general feeling among them. Am I right?

ASLAKSEN. Yes, I think I may say that I do, Burgomaster.

BURGOMASTER. Well—if there's such a praiseworthy spirit of self-sacrifice among the poorer citizens of the town, I——

ASLAKSEN. How so?

HOVSTAD. Self-sacrifice?

BURGOMASTER. It's an admirable instance of public spirit—a most admirable instance. I admit it's more than I should quite have expected. But, of course, you know public feeling better than I do.

ASLAKSEN. Yes but, Burgomaster——

BURGOMASTER. And assuredly it's no small sacrifice the town will have to make.

HOVSTAD. The town?

ASLAKSEN. But I don't understand—it's the Baths——

BURGOMASTER. At a rough provisional estimate, the alterations the Doctor thinks desirable will come to two or three hundred thousand crowns.

ASLAKSEN. That's a lot of money; but——

BURGOMASTER. Of course we shall be obliged to raise a municipal loan.

HOVSTAD (*rising*). You don't suppose that the town——?

ASLAKSEN. Would you come upon the rates? Upon the scanty savings of the lower middle-class?

BURGOMASTER. Why, my dear Mr. Aslaksen, where else are the funds to come from?

ASLAKSEN. That the shareholders in the Baths must look to.

BURGOMASTER. The shareholders are not in a position to go to further expense.

ASLAKSEN. Are you quite sure of that, Burgomaster?

BURGOMASTER. I have positive information. So if these extensive alterations are called for, the town itself will have to bear the cost.

ASLAKSEN. Oh, plague take it all!—I beg your pardon!—but this is quite another matter, **Mr. Hovstad.**

HOVSTAD. Yes, it certainly is.

BURGOMASTER. The worst of it is, that we shall be obliged to close the establishment for a couple of years.

HOVSTAD. To close it? Completely?

ASLAKSEN. For two years!

BURGOMASTER. Yes, the work will require that time at least.

ASLAKSEN. But, damn it all! we can't stand that, Burgomaster. What are we householders to live on in the meantime?

BURGOMASTER. It's extremely difficult to say, Mr. Aslaksen. But what can you do? Do you think a single visitor will come here if we go about making them fancy that the water is poisoned, that the place is pestilential, that the whole town——

ASLAKSEN. And it's all nothing but fancy?

BURGOMASTER. With the best will in the world, I've failed to convince myself that it's anything else.

ASLAKSEN. But then it's quite inexcusable of Dr. Stockmann—beg pardon, Burgomaster, but——

BURGOMASTER. I'm sorry to say you're only

speaking the truth, Mr. Aslaksen. Unfortunately, my brother has always been noted for his rashness.

ASLAKSEN. And yet you were going to back him up, Mr. Hovstad!

HOVSTAD. But who could possibly have imagined that——!

BURGOMASTER. I have drawn up a short statement of the facts, as they appear from a sober-minded standpoint ; and I've intimated that any drawbacks that may possibly exist can no doubt be remedied by measures compatible with the finances of the Baths.

HOVSTAD. Have you the article with you, Burgomaster ?

BURGOMASTER (*searching in his pockets*). Yes ; I brought it with me in case you——

ASLAKSEN (*quickly*). Plague take it, there he is !

BURGOMASTER. Who ? My brother ?

HOVSTAD. Where ? where ?

ASLAKSEN. He's coming through the printing-room.

BURGOMASTER. What a nuisance! I don't want to meet him here, and yet there are several things I want to talk to you about.

HOVSTAD (*pointing to the door on the right*). Go in there for a moment.

BURGOMASTER. But——?

HOVSTAD. You'll only find Billing there.

ASLAKSEN. Quick, quick, Burgomaster, he's just coming.

BURGOMASTER. Very well. Try to get rid of him quickly.

(He goes out by the door on the right, which
ASLAKSEN *opens, and closes behind him.)*

HOVSTAD. Pretend to be busy, Aslaksen.

(He sits down and writes. ASLAKSEN *turns over
a heap of newspapers on a chair, right.)*

DR. STOCKMANN *(entering from the printing-room).*
Here I am, back again. *(Puts down his hat and
stick.)*

HOVSTAD *(writing).* Already, Doctor? Make
haste with what we were speaking of, Aslaksen.
We've no time to lose to-day.

DR. STOCKMANN *(to* ASLAKSEN). No proof yet, I
hear.

ASLAKSEN *(without turning round).* No; how
could you expect it?

DR. STOCKMANN. Of course not; but you understand my impatience. I can have no rest or peace
until I see the thing in print.

HOVSTAD. Hm; it'll take a good while yet.
Don't you think so, Aslaksen?

ASLAKSEN. I'm almost afraid it will.

DR. STOCKMANN. All right, all right, my good
friends; then I'll look in again. I'll look in twice if
necessary. With so much at stake—the welfare of
the whole town—upon my word, it's no time for
idling. *(Is on the point of going, but stops and comes
back.)* Oh, look here, there's one other thing I must
speak to you about.

HOVSTAD. Excuse me; wouldn't some other
time——?

DR. STOCKMANN. I can tell you in two words.
You see it's this: when people read my statement

in the paper to-morrow, and find I've spent the whole winter working quietly for the good of the town——

HOVSTAD. Yes but, Doctor——

DR. STOCKMANN. I know what you're going to say. You don't think it was a bit more than my duty—my simple duty as a citizen. Of course I know that, as well as you do. But you see, my fellow-citizens—good Lord! the poor souls think so much of me——

ASLAKSEN. Yes, the townspeople have thought very highly of you till to-day, Doctor.

DR. STOCKMANN. That's exactly why I'm afraid that,—what I wanted to say was this: when all this comes to them—especially to the poorer class—as a summons to take the affairs of the town into their own hands for the future——

HOVSTAD (*rising*). Hm, Doctor, I won't conceal from you——

DR. STOCKMANN. Aha! I thought there was something brewing! But I won't hear of it. If they're going to get up anything——

HOVSTAD. How so?

DR. STOCKMANN. Well, anything of any sort—a procession with banners, or a banquet, or a subscription for a testimonial, or whatever it may be—you must give me your solemn promise to put a stop to it. And you too, Mr. Aslaksen; do you hear?

HOVSTAD. Excuse me, Doctor; we may as well tell you the whole truth first as last——

(*Enter* MRS. STOCKMANN.)

MRS. STOCKMANN (*seeing the* DOCTOR). Ah! just as I thought!

HOVSTAD (*going towards her*). Mrs. Stockmann, too?

DR. STOCKMANN. What the devil have you come here for, Katrine?

MRS. STOCKMANN. You must know well enough what I've come for.

HOVSTAD. Won't you sit down? Or perhaps—— ?

MRS. STOCKMANN. Thanks; please don't trouble. And you mustn't blame me for coming here after Stockmann, for you must remember I'm the mother of three children.

DR. STOCKMANN. Stuff and nonsense! We all know that well enough!

MRS. STOCKMANN. It doesn't look as if you thought very much about your wife and children to-day, or you wouldn't be so ready to plunge us all into misfortune.

DR. STOCKMANN. Are you quite mad, Katrine? Mayn't a man with a wife and children proclaim the truth? Mayn't he do his utmost to be an active and useful citizen? Mayn't he do his duty by the town he lives in?

MRS. STOCKMANN. Everything in moderation, Thomas.

ASLAKSEN. That's just what I say. Moderation in everything.

MRS. STOCKMANN. You're doing us a great wrong, Mr. Hovstad, in enticing my husband away from house and home, and befooling him in this way——

HOVSTAD. I have befooled no one——

DR. STOCKMANN. Befooled ! Do you think I should let myself be befooled ?

MRS. STOCKMANN. Yes, but you do. I know very well that you're the cleverest man in the town ; but you're so easily made a fool of, Thomas. (*To* HOVSTAD.) Remember he's to lose his post at the Baths if you print what he's written——

ASLAKSEN. What !

HOVSTAD. Well, really, Doctor——

DR. STOCKMANN (*laughing*). Ha ha ! just let them try ! No no, my dear, they'll think twice about that ! I have the compact majority behind me, you see.

MRS. STOCKMANN. That's just the misfortune, that you should have such a horrid thing behind you.

DR. STOCKMANN. Nonsense, Katrine ;—you go home and look after your house, and let me take care of society. How can you be in such a fright when you see me so confident and happy ? (*Rubbing his hands and walking up and down.*) Truth and the People must win the day ; of that you may be sure. Ah ! I can see the whole democracy arrayed as one triumphant host——! (*Stopping by a chair.*) Why, what the devil is that ?

ASLAKSEN (*looking at it*). Oh Lord !

HOVSTAD (*the same*). Hm !

DR. STOCKMANN. Why, here's the top-knot of authority!

(*He takes the* BURGOMASTER'S *official cap carefully between the tips of his fingers and holds it up.*)

MRS. STOCKMANN. The Burgomaster's cap !

DR. STOCKMANN. And here's the staff of office, too! But how in the devil's name did they—— ?

HOVSTAD. Well then——

DR. STOCKMANN. Ah! I understand. He's been here to talk you over. Ha ha! He brought his pigs to the wrong market! And when he caught sight of me in the printing-room—(*bursts out laughing*)—he took to his heels, eh, Mr. Aslaksen?

ASLAKSEN (*hurriedly*). Exactly; he took to his heels, Doctor.

DR. STOCKMANN. Made off without his stick and—— Fiddle-faddle! Peter never left anything behind him. But where the devil have you stowed him? Ah!—in there, of course. Now you shall see, Katrine!

MRS. STOCKMANN. Thomas—I beg you· —— !

ASLAKSEN. Take care, Doctor!

(DR. STOCKMANN *has put on the* BURGOMASTER'S *cap and grasped his stick; he now goes up to the door, throws it open, and makes a military salute. The* BURGOMASTER *enters, red with anger. Behind him comes* BILLING.)

BURGOMASTER. What's the meaning of this folly?

DR. STOCKMANN. Respect, my good Peter! Now, it's I that am in power in this town.

(*He struts up and down.*)

MRS. STOCKMANN (*almost crying*). Oh, Thomas——!

BURGOMASTER (*following him*). Give me my cap and stick!

DR. STOCKMANN (*as before*). You may be Chief of Police, but I'm Burgomaster. I'm master of the whole town, I tell you!

BURGOMASTER. Put down my cap, I say. Remember it's an official cap, as by law prescribed.

DR. STOCKMANN. Pshaw! Do you think the awakening lion of the democracy will let itself be scared by a uniform cap? There's to be a revolution in the town to-morrow, let me tell you. You threatened me with dismissal; but now I dismiss you —dismiss you from all your offices of trust. You think I can't do it?—Oh yes, I can! I have the irresistible forces of society with me. Hovstad and Billing will thunder in the *People's Messenger*, and Aslaksen will take the field at the head of the whole Householders' Association——

ASLAKSEN. I shall not, Doctor.

DR. STOCKMANN. Surely you will——

BURGOMASTER. Aha! Perhaps Mr. Hovstad would like to join the agitation after all?

HOVSTAD. No, Burgomaster.

ASLAKSEN. No, Mr. Hovstad isn't such a fool as to ruin both himself and the paper for the sake of fancy.

DR. STOCKMANN (*looking about him*). What does all this mean?

HOVSTAD. You have presented your case in a false light, Doctor ; therefore I'm unable to give you my support.

BILLING. And after what the Burgomaster has been so kind as to explain to me, I——

DR. STOCKMANN. In a false light! Well, I'm responsible for that. Just you print my article, and you'll see I'll prove it up to the hilt.

HOVSTAD. I shall not print it. I cannot, and will not, and dare not print it.

DR. STOCKMANN. You dare not? What nonsense! You're editor; and I suppose it's the editor that directs a paper.

ASLAKSEN. No, it's the readers, Doctor.

BILLING. Luckily, it is.

ASLAKSEN. It's public opinion, the intelligent majority, the householders, and all the rest. It's they who direct a paper.

DR. STOCKMANN (*calmly*). And all these powers I have against me?

ASLAKSEN. Yes, you have. It would be absolute ruin for the town if your article were inserted.

DR. STOCKMANN. Indeed!

BURGOMASTER. My hat and stick! (DR. STOCK-MANN *takes off the cap and lays it on the table along with the stick. The* BURGOMASTER *takes them both.*) Your term of office has come to an untimely end.

DR. STOCKMANN. The end is not yet. (*To* HOVSTAD.) So it's quite impossible to print my paper in the *Messenger?*

HOVSTAD. Quite impossible; for the sake of your family, if for no other reason.

MRS. STOCKMANN. Oh, please leave his family out of the question, Mr. Hovstad.

BURGOMASTER (*takes a manuscript from his pocket*). When this appears, the public will be in possession of all necessary information; it's an authentic statement. Here it is.

HOVSTAD (*taking the MS.*). Good! It shall certainly be inserted.

DR. STOCKMANN. And not mine! You imagine you can kill me and the truth by a conspiracy of silence! But it won't be so easy as you think. Mr Aslaksen, will you be good enough to print my article at once, as a pamphlet? I'll pay for it and be my own publisher. I'll have five hundred copies—no, I'll have six hundred.

ASLAKSEN. No. If you offered me its weight in gold I shouldn't dare to lend my press to such a purpose, Doctor. I daren't fly in the face of public opinion. You won't get it printed anywhere in the whole town.

DR. STOCKMANN. Then give it me back.

HOVSTAD (*handing him the MS.*). By all means.

DR. STOCKMANN (*taking up his hat and cane*). It shall be made public all the same. I'll read it at a mass meeting; all my fellow-citizens shall hear the voice of truth!

BURGOMASTER. Not a single society in the town would let you their hall for such a purpose.

ASLAKSEN. Not one, I'm quite certain.

BILLING. No, strike me dead if they would!

MRS. STOCKMANN. That would be too disgraceful! But why is every one against you like this?

DR. STOCKMANN (*angrily*). Ah, I'll tell you. It's because in this town all the men are old women—like you. They all think of nothing but their families, not of the general good.

MRS. STOCKMANN (*taking his arm*). Then I'll show them that an—an old woman can be a man, for once in a way. For *now* I'll stand by you, Thomas.

DR. STOCKMANN. Bravely said, Katrine! My word for it, the truth shall out! If they won't let me a hall, I'll hire a drum and march through the town with it; and I'll read my paper at every street corner.

BURGOMASTER. Surely you're not such a raving lunatic as that?

DR. STOCKMANN. I am.

ASLAKSEN. You wouldn't get a single man in the whole town to go with you.

BILLING. No, strike me dead if you would.

MRS. STOCKMANN. Don't give in, Thomas. I'll send the boys with you.

DR. STOCKMANN. That's a splendid idea!

MRS. STOCKMANN. Morten 'll be delighted; and Eilif 'll go too, I'm sure.

DR. STOCKMANN. Yes, and so will Petra. And you yourself, Katrine!

MRS. STOCKMANN. No no, not I. But I'll stand at the window and watch you—that I will.

DR. STOCKMANN (*throwing his arms about her and kissing her*). Thanks, thanks! Now, my good sirs, we're ready for the fight! Now we'll see if your poltroonery can close the mouth of the patriot who would purge society.

(*He and his wife go out together by the door in the back, left.*)

BURGOMASTER (*shaking his head dubiously*). Now he's driven *her* mad too!

Act Fourth.

(A large old-fashioned room in CAPTAIN HORSTER'S *house. An open folding-door in the background leads to an anteroom. Three windows, left. About the middle of the opposite wall is a platform, and on it a small table, two candles, a water-bottle and glass, and a bell. The rest of the room is lighted by sconces placed between the windows. In front, on the left, is a table with a candle on it, and by it a chair. In front, to the right, a door, and near it a few chairs.)*

(Large meeting of all classes of townsfolk. In the crowd are a few women and school-boys. More and more people gradually stream in from the back until the room is quite full.)

1ST CITIZEN *(to another standing near him)*. So you're here too, Lamstad?

2ND CITIZEN. I always go to every meeting.

A BYSTANDER. I suppose you've brought your whistle?

2ND CITIZEN. Of course I have; haven't you?

3RD CITIZEN. Rather. And Skipper Evensen said he'd bring a great big horn.

2ND CITIZEN. He's a good one, is Evensen! *(Laughter in the group.)*

4TH CITIZEN *(joining them)*. I say, what's it all about? What's going on here to-night?

2ND CITIZEN. Why, it's Dr. Stockmann that's going to lecture against the Burgomaster.

4TH CITIZEN. But the Burgomaster's his brother.

1ST CITIZEN. That doesn't matter. Dr. Stockmann's not afraid of him.

3RD CITIZEN. But he's all wrong; the *People's Messenger* says so.

2ND CITIZEN. Yes, he must be wrong this time; for neither the Householders' Association nor the Citizens' Club would let him have a hall.

1ST CITIZEN. They wouldn't even let him have the hall at the Baths.

2ND CITIZEN. No, you may be sure they wouldn't.

A MAN (*in another group*). Now, who's the one to follow in this business, eh?

ANOTHER MAN (*in the same group*). Just keep your eye on Aslaksen, and do as he does.

BILLING (*with a writing-case under his arm, makes his way through the crowd*). Excuse me, gentlemen. Will you allow me to pass? I'm here to report for the *People's Messenger*. Many thanks.

(*Sits by the table on the left.*)

A WORKING-MAN. Who's he?

ANOTHER WORKING-MAN. Don't you know him? It's that fellow Billing, that writes for Aslaksen's paper.

(CAPTAIN HORSTER *enters by the right-hand door, escorting* MRS. STOCKMANN *and* PETRA. EILIF *and* MORTEN *follow them.*)

HORSTER. This is where I thought you might sit; you can so easily slip out if anything should happen.

MRS. STOCKMANN. Do you think there'll be any disturbance?

HORSTER. One can never tell—with such a crowd But there's no need to be anxious.

MRS. STOCKMANN (*sitting down*). How kind it was of you to offer Stockmann this room!

HORSTER. As no one else would, I——

PETRA (*who has also seated herself*). And it was brave too, Horster.

HORSTER. Oh, I don't see that it needed much courage.

(HOVSTAD *and* ASLAKSEN *enter at the same moment, but make their way through the crowd separately.*)

ASLAKSEN (*going towards* HORSTER). Hasn't the Doctor come yet?

HORSTER. He's waiting in there.

(*A movement at the door in the background.*)

HOVSTAD (*to* BILLING). There's the Burgomaster, look!

BILLING. Yes, strike me dead if he hasn't come to the fore after all!

(BURGOMASTER STOCKMANN *makes his way blandly through the meeting, bowing politely to both sides, and takes his stand by the wall on the left. Immediately afterwards,* DR. STOCK-MANN *enters by the door on the right. He wears a black frock-coat and white necktie. Faint applause, met by a subdued hissing. Then silence.*)

DR. STOCKMANN (*in a low tone*). How do you feel, Katrine?

MRS. STOCKMANN. Oh, I'm all right. (*In a low voice.*) Now do keep your temper, Thomas.

DR. STOCKMANN. Oh, I'll keep myself well in hand. (*Looks at his watch, ascends the platform, and bows.*)   It's a quarter past the hour, so I'll begin——

(*Takes out his MS.*)

ASLAKSEN.   But I suppose a chairman must be elected first.

DR. STOCKMANN.   No ; there's no necessity.

SEVERAL GENTLEMEN (*shouting*).   Yes, yes.

BURGOMASTER.   I should certainly say that a chairman ought to be elected.

DR. STOCKMANN.   But I've called this meeting to give a lecture, Peter !

BURGOMASTER.   Dr. Stockmann's lecture may possibly lead to differences of opinion.

SEVERAL VOICES IN THE CROWD.   A chairman ! a chairman !

HOVSTAD.   The general voice of the meeting seems to be for a chairman.

DR. STOCKMANN (*controlling himself*).   Very well then ; let the meeting have its way.

ASLAKSEN.   Will not the Burgomaster take the chair?

THREE GENTLEMEN (*clapping*).   Bravo ! Bravo !

BURGOMASTER.   For reasons you will easily understand, I must decline.   But, fortunately, we have among us one whom I think we can all accept.   I allude to the president of the Householders' Association, Mr. Aslaksen.

MANY VOICES.   Yes, yes !   Long live Aslaksen ! Hurrah for Aslaksen !

(DR. STOCKMANN *takes his MS. and descends from the platform.*)

ASLAKSEN.   If my fellow-citizens call upon me, I cannot refuse to——

(*Applause and cheers.* ASLAKSEN *ascends the platform.*)

BILLING (*writing*) So—"Mr. Aslaksen was elected by acclamation——"

ASLAKSEN. And now, as I have been called to the chair, I take the liberty of saying a few brief words. I am a quiet, peace-loving man ; I am in favour of discreet moderation, and of—and of moderate discretion. Every one who knows me, knows that.

MANY VOICES. Yes, yes, Aslaksen !

ASLAKSEN. I have learnt in the school of life and of experience that moderation is the virtue in which the individual citizen finds his best advantage——

BURGOMASTER. Hear, hear !

ASLAKSEN. ——and it is discretion and moderation, too, that best serve the community. I will therefore beg our respected fellow-citizen, who has called this meeting, to keep within the bounds of moderation.

A MAN (*by the door*). Three cheers for the Temperance Society !

A VOICE. Go to the devil !

VOICES. Hush ! hush !

ASLAKSEN. No interruptions, gentlemen ! Does any one wish to offer any observations ?

BURGOMASTER. Mr. Chairman !

ASLAKSEN. Burgomaster Stockmann will address the meeting.

BURGOMASTER. On account of my close relationship—of which you are probably aware—to the present medical officer of the Baths, I should have preferred not to speak here this evening. But my position with regard to the Baths, and my care for the most important interests of this town, force me to move a resolution. I may doubtless assume that not a single citizen here present thinks it desirable that untrustworthy and exaggerated statements should get abroad as to the sanitary condition of the Baths and of our town.

MANY VOICES. No, no! Certainly not! We protest!

BURGOMASTER. I therefore beg to move, "That this meeting declines to hear the proposed lecture or speech on the subject by the medical officer of the Baths."

DR. STOCKMANN (*flaring up*). Declines to hear! What do you mean?

MRS. STOCKMANN (*coughing*). Hm! hm!

DR. STOCKMANN (*controlling himself*). So I'm not to be heard?

BURGOMASTER. In my statement in the *People's Messenger* I have made the public acquainted with the essential facts, so that all well-disposed citizens can easily draw their own conclusions. From that statement you will see that the medical officer's proposal—besides amounting to a vote of censure against the leading men of the town—at bottom only means saddling the ratepayers with an unnecessary expense of at least a hundred thousand crowns.

(*Protestations and some hissing.*)

ASLAKSEN (*ringing the bell*). Order, gentlemen! I must beg leave to support the Burgomaster's resolution. I quite agree with him that there is something beneath the surface of the Doctor's agitation. In all his talk about the Baths, it is really a revolution he is aiming at; he wants to effect a redistribution of power. No one doubts the excellence of Dr. Stockmann's intentions—of course there can't be two opinions as to that. I, too, am in favour of self-government by the people, if only it doesn't cost the ratepayers too much. But in this case it would do so; and therefore I—confound it all—I beg your pardon—I cannot go with Dr. Stockmann upon this occasion. You can buy even gold too dear; that's my opinion.

(*Loud applause on all sides.*)

HOVSTAD. I also feel bound to explain my attitude. In the beginning, Dr. Stockmann's agitation seemed to find favour in several quarters, and I supported it as impartially as I could. But then we found we had been misled by a false statement——

DR. STOCKMANN. False——!

HOVSTAD. Well then, an untrustworthy statement. This the Burgomaster's report has proved. I trust no one here present doubts my liberal principles; the attitude of the *Messenger* on all great political questions is well known to you all. But I have learned from experienced and thoughtful men that in purely local matters a paper must observe a certain amount of caution.

ASLAKSEN. I quite agree with the speaker.

HOVSTAD. And in the matter under discussion it is evident that Dr. Stockmann has public opinion against him. But, gentlemen, what is the first and foremost duty of an editor? Is it not to work in harmony with his readers? Has he not in some sort received a tacit mandate to further assiduously and unweariedly the interests of his constituents? Or am I mistaken in this?

MANY VOICES. No, no, no! Hovstad is right!

HOVSTAD. It has cost me a bitter struggle to break with a man in whose house I have of late been a frequent guest—with a man who up to this day has enjoyed the universal goodwill of his fellow-citizens— with a man whose only, or, at any rate, whose chief fault is that he consults his heart rather than his head.

A FEW SCATTERED VOICES. That's true! Hurrah for Dr. Stockmann!

HOVSTAD. But my duty towards the community has forced me to break with him. Then, too, there is another consideration that impels me to oppose him, and, if possible, to bar the fatal path upon which he is entering: consideration for his family——

DR. STOCKMANN. Keep to the water-works and sewers!

HOVSTAD. ——consideration for his wife and his unprotected[1] children.

MORTEN. Is that us, mother?

MRS. STOCKMANN. Hush!

ASLAKSEN. I will now put the Burgomaster's resolution to the vote.

DR. STOCKMANN. It's not necessary. I shan't say anything this evening of all the filth at the Baths. No! You shall hear something quite different.

BURGOMASTER (*half aloud*). What next, I wonder?

_____
[1] Literally, "unprovided-for."

A DRUNKEN MAN (*at the main entrance*). I'm a ratepayer, so I've a right to my opinion! It's my full, firm, incomprehensible opinion that——

SEVERAL VOICES. Silence, up there!

OTHERS. He's drunk! Turn him out!

(*The drunken man is turned out.*)

DR. STOCKMANN. Can I speak?

ASLAKSEN (*ringing the bell*). Dr. Stockmann will address the meeting.

DR. STOCKMANN. A few days ago I should have liked to see any one venture upon such an attempt to gag me as has been made here to-night! I would have fought like a lion for my sacred rights. But now I scarcely care, for now I have more important things to speak of. (*The people crowd closer round him. MORTEN KIIL comes in sight among the bystanders. DR. STOCKMANN continues.*) During the last few days I have been thinking and thinking of so many things, that at last my head seemed to be in a whirl——

BURGOMASTER (*coughing*). Hm!

DR. STOCKMANN. ——but presently my ideas clarified, and I soon got the hang of the whole matter. That's why I stand here this evening. I am about to make great revelations, my fellow-citizens! I am going to announce to you a far more important discovery than the trifling fact that our water-works are poisoned, and that our health-resort is built on pestilential ground.

MANY VOICES (*shouting*). Don't speak about the Baths! We won't listen to that! No more of that!

DR. STOCKMANN. I have said I would speak of

the great discovery I have made within the last few days—the discovery that all our sources of spiritual life are poisoned, and that our whole society rests upon a pestilential basis of falsehood.

SEVERAL VOICES (*in astonishment and half aloud*). What's he saying?

BURGOMASTER. Such an insinuation——

ASLAKSEN (*with his hand on the bell*). I must call upon the speaker to moderate his expressions.

DR. STOCKMANN. I have loved my native town as dearly as man could love the home of his childhood. I was young when I left our town, and distance, home-sickness, and memory threw, as it were, a glamour over the place and its people. (*Some clapping and shouts of approval.*) Then for years I was imprisoned in a horrible hole, far away in the north. As I went about among the people scattered here and there over the stony wilderness, it seemed to me, many a time, that these poor degraded creatures ought to have had a cattle-doctor to attend them rather than a man like me.

(*Murmurs in the room.*)

BILLING (*laying down his pen*). Strike me dead if I've ever heard——!

HOVSTAD. What an insult to a worthy peasantry!

DR. STOCKMANN. Wait a moment!— I don't think any one can reproach me with forgetting my native town up there. I sat brooding like an eider-duck, and what I hatched was—the plan of the Baths. (*Applause and interruptions.*) And when, at last, fate ordered things so happily that I could come home again—then, fellow-citizens, it seemed to me that I hadn't another desire in the world. Yes, one desire I had : an eager, constant, burning desire to be of service to my birthplace, and to its people.

BURGOMASTER (*looking into vacancy*). A strange method to select—hm !

DR. STOCKMANN. So I went about revelling in my happy illusions. But yesterday morning—no, it was really two nights ago—my mind's eyes were opened wide, and the first thing I saw was the extraordinary stupidity of the authorities——

(*Noise, cries, and laughter.* MRS. STOCKMANN *coughs emphatically.*)

BURGOMASTER. Mr. Chairman !

ASLAKSEN (*ringing his bell*). In virtue of my position——!

DR. STOCKMANN. It's petty to catch me up on a word, Mr. Aslaksen. I only meant that I became alive to the extraordinary muddle the leading men had been guilty of down at the Baths. I detest leading men—I've seen enough of them in my time. They're like goats in a young plantation: they do harm everywhere ; they block the path of a free man wherever he turns—and I should be glad if we could exterminate them like other noxious animals——

(*Uproar in the room.*)

BURGOMASTER. Mr. Chairman, are such expressions permissible ?

ASLAKSEN (*with his hand on the bell*). Doctor Stockmann——!

DR. STOCKMANN. I can't conceive how it is that I've only now seen through these gentry; for haven't

I had a magnificent example before my eyes here every day—my brother Peter—slow of understanding, tenacious in prejudice——

(*Laughter, noise, and whistling.* MRS. STOCK-MANN *coughs.* ASLAKSEN *rings violently.*)

THE DRUNKEN MAN (*who has come in again*). Is it me you're alluding to? Sure enough, my name's Pettersen; but devil take me if——

ANGRY VOICES. Out with that drunken man! Turn him out!

(*The man is again turned out.*)

BURGOMASTER. Who is that person?

A BYSTANDER. I don't know him, Burgomaster.

ANOTHER. He doesn't belong to the town.

A THIRD. I believe he's a timber-merchant from——

(*The rest is inaudible.*)

ASLAKSEN. The man was evidently intoxicated. Continue, Dr. Stockmann; but do strive to be moderate.

DR. STOCKMANN. Well, fellow-citizens, I'll say no more about our leading men. If any one imagines, from what I've just said, that I want to make short work of these gentlemen to-night, he's mistaken—altogether mistaken. For I cherish the comforting belief that these laggards, these relics of a decaying order of thought, are diligently cutting their own throats. They need no doctor to hasten their end. And these are not the people that constitute the most serious danger to society; it is not they who are most active in poisoning our spiritual life and making a plague-spot of the ground beneath our feet; it is not they who are the most dangerous enemies of truth and freedom in our society.

CRIES FROM ALL SIDES. Who, then? Who is it? Name, name!

DR. STOCKMANN. Yes, you may be sure I'll name them! For *this* is the great discovery I made yesterday! (*In a louder tone.*) The most dangerous foe to truth and freedom in our midst is the compact majority. Yes, it's the confounded, compact, liberal majority! There, I've told you!

> (*Immense disturbance in the room. Most of the audience are shouting, stamping, and whistling. Several elderly gentlemen exchange furtive glances and seem to be enjoying the scene.* MRS. STOCKMANN *rises nervously.* EILIF *and* MORTEN *advance threateningly towards the school-boys, who are making a noise.* ASLAKSEN *rings the bell and calls for order.* HOVSTAD *and* BILLING *both speak, but nothing can be heard. At last quiet is restored.*)

ASLAKSEN. I request the speaker to withdraw his ill-considered expressions.

DR. STOCKMANN. Never, Mr. Aslaksen! For it's this very majority that robs me of my freedom, and wants to forbid me to speak the truth.

HOVSTAD. Right is always on the side of the majority.

BILLING. Yes, and truth too, strike me dead!

DR. STOCKMANN. The majority is never right. Never, I say! That's one of the social lies a free, thinking man is bound to rebel against. Who make up the majority in any given country? Is it the wise men or the fools? I think we must agree that the fools are in a terrible, overwhelming majority, all the wide world over. But how the deuce can it ever be right for the fools to rule over the wise men? (*Noise and shouts.*) Yes yes, you can shout me down, but you cannot gainsay me. The majority has might—unhappily—but right it has not. I and the few, the individuals, are right. The minority is always right.

(*Renewed disturbances.*)

HOVSTAD. Ha ha! So Dr. Stockmann has turned aristocrat since the day before yesterday.

DR. STOCKMANN. I have said that I won't waste a word on the little, narrow-chested, short-winded crew that lie in our wake. Pulsating life has nothing more to do with them. I will rather speak of the few individuals among us who have made all the new, germinating truths their own. These men stand, as it were, at the outposts, so far in the van that the compact majority has not yet reached them—and *there* they fight for truths that are too lately born into the world's consciousness to have won over the majority.

HOVSTAD. So the Doctor's a revolutionist now.

DR. STOCKMANN. Yes, by Heaven, I am, Mr. Hovstad! I'm going to revolt against the lie that truth resides in the majority. What sort of truths do the majority rally round? Truths that are decrepit with age. When a truth is so old as that it's in a fair way to become a lie, gentlemen. (*Laughter and jeers.*) Yes yes; you may believe me or not, as you please; but truths are by no means the wiry Methusalehs some people think them. A normally-constituted truth lives—let me say—as a rule, seventeen or eighteen years; at the outside twenty; seldom longer. And truths so stricken in years are always shockingly thin; yet it's not till then that the majority takes them up and recommends them to society as wholesome food. I can assure you there's not much nutriment in that sort of fare; you may take my word as a doctor for that. All these majority-truths are like last year's salt pork; they're like rancid, mouldy ham, producing all the moral scurvy that devastates society.

ASLAKSEN. It seems to me that the honourable speaker is wandering rather far from the subject.

BURGOMASTER. I beg to endorse the Chairman's remark.

DR. STOCKMANN. Why you're surely mad, Peter! I'm keeping as closely to my text as I possibly can, for my text is just this—that the masses, the majority, that confounded compact majority—it's that, I say, that's poisoning our spiritual life at its source, and making a plague-spot of the ground beneath our feet.

HOVSTAD. And you make this charge against the great, independent majority, just because they're sensible enough to accept only certain and acknowledged truths?

DR. STOCKMANN. Ah, my dear Mr. Hovstad, don't talk about certain truths! The truths acknowledged by the masses, the multitude, were certain truths to the vanguard in our grandfathers' days. We, the vanguard of to-day, don't acknowledge them any longer; and I don't believe there's any other certain truth but this—that no society can live a healthy life upon such old, marrowless truths as these.

HOVSTAD. But instead of all this vague talk, suppose you were to give us some specimens of these old marrowless truths that we're living upon.

(*Approval from several quarters.*)

DR. STOCKMANN. Oh, I can't go over the whole rubbish-heap; so, for the present, I'll keep to one acknowledged truth, which is a hideous lie at bottom, but which Mr. Hovstad, and the *Messenger*, and all adherents of the *Messenger*, live on all the same.

HOVSTAD. And that is——?

DR. STOCKMANN. That is the doctrine you've inherited from our forefathers, and go on heedlessly proclaiming far and wide—the doctrine that the multitude, the vulgar herd, the masses, are the pith of the people—that they *are* the people—that the common man, the ignorant, undeveloped member of society, has the same right to condemn and to sanction, to counsel and to govern, as the intellectually distinguished few.

BILLING. Well, now, strike me dead——!

HOVSTAD (*shouting at the same time*). Citizens, please note that!

ANGRY VOICES. Ho-ho! Aren't we the people? Is it only the grand folks that are to govern?

A WORKING MAN. Turn out the fellow that talks like that!

OTHERS. Turn him out!

A CITIZEN (*shouting*). Now for your horn, Evensen.

(*The deep notes of a horn are heard; whistling, and terrific noise in the room.*)

DR. STOCKMANN (*when the noise has somewhat*

subsided). Now do be reasonable! Can't you bear to hear the voice of truth for once? I don't ask you all to agree with me straight away. But I certainly should have thought that Mr. Hovstad would have backed me up, when he'd collected himself a bit. Mr. Hovstad calls himself a free-thinker——

SEVERAL VOICES (*subdued and wondering*). Free-thinker, did he say? What? Mr. Hovstad a free-thinker?

HOVSTAD (*shouting*). Prove it, Dr. Stockmann! When have I said so in print?

DR. STOCKMANN (*reflecting*). No, on my soul you're right there; you've never had the frankness to do that. Well, I won't get you into a scrape, Mr. Hovstad. Let me be the free-thinker then. And now I'll make it clear to you all, and on scientific grounds, that the *Messenger* is leading you shamefully by the nose, when it tells you that you, the masses, the crowd, are the true pith of the people. You see that's only a newspaper lie. The masses are nothing but the raw material that must be fashioned into the People. (*Murmurs, laughter, and disturbance in the room.*) Is it not so with all other living creatures? What a difference between a cultivated and an un-cultivated breed of animals! Only look at a common barn-door hen. What meat do you get from such a skinny carcase? Not much, I can tell you! And what sort of eggs does she lay? A decent crow or raven can lay nearly as good. Then take a cultivated Spanish or Japanese hen, or take a fine pheasant or turkey—ah! then you'll see the difference. And now look at the dog, our near relation. Think first of an ordinary vulgar cur—I mean one of those wretched, ragged, low mongrels that haunt the gutters, and soil the side-walks. Then place such a mongrel by the side of a poodle-dog, descended through many generations from an aristocratic strain, who has lived on delicate food, and has heard harmonious voices and music. Do you think the brain of the poodle hasn't developed quite differently from that of the mongrel? Yes, you may be sure it has! It's well-bred poodle-pups like this that jugglers train to perform the most extraordinary tricks. A common peasant-cur could never learn anything of the sort—not if he tried till doomsday.

(*Noise and laughter are heard all round.*)

A CITIZEN (*shouting*). Do you want to make dogs of us now?

ANOTHER MAN. We're not animals, Doctor.

DR. STOCKMANN. Yes, on my soul, but we are animals, my good sir! We're one and all of us animals, whether we like it or not. But truly there aren't many aristocratic animals among us. Ah! there's a terrible difference between men-poodles and men-mongrels. And the ridiculous part of it is, that Mr. Hovstad quite agrees with me so long as it's four-legged animals we're talking of——

HOVSTAD. Oh, let them alone.

DR. STOCKMANN. All right—but so soon as I apply the law to two-legged animals, Mr. Hovstad stops short; then he daren't hold his own opinions, or think out his own thoughts; then he turns all his knowledge topsy-turvy, and proclaims in the *People's Messenger* that barn-door hens and gutter mongrels are precisely the finest specimens' in the menagerie. But that's always the way, so long as you haven't worked the commonness out of your system, and fought your way up to spiritual distinction.

HOVSTAD. I make no pretensions to any sort of distinction. I come of simple peasant stock, and I'm proud that my root lies deep down among the common people, who are now being jeered at.

SEVERAL WORKMEN. Hurrah for Hovstad! Hurrah! hurrah!

DR. STOCKMANN. The sort of common people I'm speaking of are not found among the lower classes alone; they crawl and swarm all around us— up to the very summits of society. Just look at your own smug, respectable Burgomaster! Why, my brother Peter belongs as clearly to the common people as any man that walks on two legs——

(*Laughter and hisses.*)

BURGOMASTER. I protest against such personalities.

DR. STOCKMANN (*imperturbably*). ——and that not because, like myself, he's descended from a good-for-nothing old pirate from Pomerania, or thereabouts— for that's our ancestry——

BURGOMASTER. An absurd tradition! Utterly groundless.

DR. STOCKMANN. ——but he is so because he thinks the thoughts and holds the opinions of his official superiors. Men who do that belong, intellec-tually-speaking, to the mob; and that's why my distinguished brother Peter is at bottom so undis-tinguished,—and consequently so illiberal.

BURGOMASTER. Mr. Chairman——

HOVSTAD. So that the distinguished people in this country are the liberals? That's quite a new light on the subject. (*Laughter.*)

DR. STOCKMANN. Yes, that's part of my new discovery. And this, too, follows, that liberality of thought is almost precisely the same thing as morality. Therefore I say it's altogether unpardonable of the *Messenger* to proclaim day after day the false doctrine that it's the masses, the multitude, the compact majority, that monopolise liberality and morality,— and that vice and corruption and all sorts of spiritual uncleanness ooze out of culture, as all that filth oozes down to the Baths from the Mill Dale tan-works! (*Noise and interruptions.* DR. STOCKMANN *goes on imperturbably, smiling in his eagerness.*) And yet this same *Messenger* can preach about raising the masses and the multitude to a higher level of life! Why, deuce take it, if the *Messenger's* own doctrine holds good, the elevation of the masses would simply mean hurling them into destruction! But, happily, it's only an old traditional lie that culture demoralises. No, it's stupidity, poverty, the ugliness of life, that do the devil's work! In a house that isn't aired and swept every day—my wife Katrine maintains that the floors ought to be scrubbed too, but we can't discuss that now;—well,—in such a house, I say, within two or three years, people lose the power of thinking or acting morally. Lack of oxygen enervates the conscience. And there seems to be precious little oxygen in many and many a house in this town, since the whole compact majority is unscrupulous enough to want to found its future upon a quagmire of lies and fraud.

ASLAKSEN. I cannot allow so gross an insult to be levelled against the whole body of citizens.

A GENTLEMAN. I move that the Chairman order the speaker to sit down.

EAGER VOICES. Yes, yes, that's right! Sit down! Sit down!

DR. STOCKMANN (*flaring up*). Then I'll proclaim the truth at every street corner! I'll write to newspapers in other towns! The whole land shall know how things go on here!

HOVSTAD. It would almost seem as if the Doctor wanted to ruin the town.

DR. STOCKMANN. Yes, I love my native town so well, I would rather ruin it than see it flourishing upon a lie.

ASLAKSEN. That's putting it strongly.

(*Noise and whistling.* MRS. STOCKMANN *coughs in vain; the* DOCTOR *no longer heeds her.*)

HOVSTAD (*shouting amid the tumult*). The man who would ruin a whole community must be an enemy to his fellow-citizens!

DR. STOCKMANN (*with growing excitement*). What does it matter if a lying community is ruined! It should be levelled to the ground, I say! All men who live upon lies should be exterminated like vermin! You'll poison the whole country in time; you'll bring it to such a pass that the whole country will deserve to perish. And if it ever comes to that, I shall say, from the bottom of my heart: Perish the country! Perish all its people!

A MAN (*in the crowd*). Why, he talks like a regular enemy of the people!

BILLING. Strike me dead but there spoke the people's voice!

THE WHOLE ASSEMBLY (*shouting*). Yes! yes! yes! He's an enemy of the people! He hates his country! He hates the people!

ASLAKSEN. Both as a citizen of this town and as a man, I am deeply shocked at what I have here had to listen to. Dr. Stockmann has unmasked himself in a manner I should never have dreamt of. I am reluctantly forced to subscribe to the opinion just expressed by some worthy citizens; and I think we ought to formulate this opinion in a resolution. I therefore beg to move, "That this meeting declares the medical officer of the Baths, Dr. Thomas Stockmann, to be an enemy of the people."

> (*Thunders of applause and cheers. Many form a circle round the* DOCTOR *and hoot at him.* MRS. STOCKMANN *and* PETRA *have risen.* MORTEN *and* EILIF *fight the other school-boys, who have also been hooting. Some grown-up persons separate them.*)

DR. STOCKMANN (*to the people hooting*). Ah! fools that you are! I tell you that——

ASLAKSEN (*ringing*). The Doctor is out of order in speaking. A formal vote must be taken; but out of consideration for personal feelings, it will be taken in writing and without names. Have you any blank paper, Mr. Billing?

BILLING. Here's both blue and white paper——

ASLAKSEN. That'll do; we can manage more

quickly this way. Tear it up. That's it. (*To the meeting.*) Blue means no, white means yes. I myself will go round and collect the votes.

(*The* BURGOMASTER *leaves the room.* ASLAKSEN *and a few others go round with pieces of paper in hats.*)

A GENTLEMAN (*to* HOVSTAD). What can be the matter with the Doctor? What does it all mean?

HOVSTAD. Why, you know how irrepressible he is.

ANOTHER GENTLEMAN (*to* BILLING). I say, you're often at his house. Have you ever noticed if the fellow drinks?

BILLING. Strike me dead if I know what to say. Toddy's always on the table when any one looks in.

A THIRD GENTLEMAN. No, I should rather say he was subject to fits of insanity.

FIRST GENTLEMAN. I wonder if madness runs in the family?

BILLING. I shouldn't be surprised.

A FOURTH GENTLEMAN. No, it's pure malice. He wants to be revenged for something.

BILLING. He was certainly talking about a rise in his salary the other day; but he didn't get it.

ALL THE GENTLEMEN (*together*). Ah! that explains everything.

THE DRUNKEN MAN (*in the crowd*). I want a blue one, I do! And I'll have a white one too!

SEVERAL PEOPLE. There's the tipsy man again! Turn him out!

MORTEN KIIL (*approaching the* DOCTOR). Well, Stockmann, you see now what this tomfoolery leads to!

DR. STOCKMANN. I've done my duty.

MORTEN KIIL. What was that you said about the Mill Dale tanneries?

DR. STOCKMANN. Why, you heard what I said—that all the filth comes from them.

MORTEN KIIL. From my tannery as well?

DR. STOCKMANN. Unfortunately, yours is about the worst of all.

MORTEN KIIL. Are you going to put that into the papers too?

DR. STOCKMANN. I can't keep anything back.

MORTEN KIIL. That may cost you dear, Stockmann!

(*He goes out.*)

A FAT GENTLEMAN (*goes up to* HORSTER, *without bowing to the ladies*). Well, Captain, so you lend your house to enemies of the people?

HORSTER. I suppose I can do as I please with my own, Sir.

THE GENTLEMAN. Then of course you can have no objection if I follow your example?

HORSTER. What do you mean, Sir?

THE GENTLEMAN. You shall hear from me to-morrow.

(*Turns away and goes out.*)

PETRA. Wasn't that the owner of your ship?

HORSTER. Yes, that was Mr. Vik.

ASLAKSEN (*with the voting papers in his hands, ascends the platform and rings*). Gentlemen! I have now to announce the result of the vote. All, with one exception——

A YOUNG GENTLEMAN. That's the tipsy man!

ASLAKSEN. With the exception of one intoxicated person, this meeting of citizens declares the medical officer of the Baths, Dr. Thomas Stockmann, to be an enemy of the people. (*Cheers and applause.*) Three cheers for our fine old municipality! (*Cheers.*) Three cheers for our able and energetic Burgomaster, who has so loyally put aside the claims of kindred! (*Cheers.*) The meeting is dissolved. (*He descends.*)

BILLING. Three cheers for the Chairman!

ALL. Hurrah for Aslaksen!

DR. STOCKMANN. My hat and coat, Petra! Captain, have you room for passengers to the new world?

HORSTER. For you and yours, Doctor, we'll make room.

DR. STOCKMANN (*while* PETRA *helps him on with his coat*). Good! Come, Katrine! come, boys!

(*He gives his wife his arm.*)

MRS. STOCKMANN (*in a low voice*). Dear Thomas, let us go out by the back way.

DR. STOCKMANN. No back ways, Katrine! (*In a loud voice.*) You shall hear from the enemy of the people before he shakes the dust from his feet! I'm not so good-natured as a certain person; I don't say: I forgive you, for you know not what you do.

ASLAKSEN (*shouts*). That is a blasphemous comparison, Dr. Stockmann!

BILLING. Strike me—— That's more than a serious man can stand!

A COARSE VOICE. And he threatens us into the bargain!

Act Fifth.

(DR. STOCKMANN'S *Study. Bookshelves and glass cases with various collections along the walls. In the back, a door leading to the anteroom; in front, on the left, a door to the sitting-room. In the wall to the right are two windows, all the panes of which are smashed. In the middle of the room is the* DOCTOR'S *writing-table, covered with books and papers. The room is in disorder. It is forenoon.*)

(DR. STOCKMANN, *in dressing-gown, slippers, and skull-cap, is bending down and raking with an umbrella under one of the cabinets; at last he rakes out a stone.*)

DR. STOCKMANN (*speaking through the sitting-room doorway*). Katrine, I've found another!

MRS. STOCKMANN (*in the sitting-room*). Oh, you'll find plenty more.

DR. STOCKMANN (*placing the stone on a pile of others on the table*). I shall keep these stones as sacred relics. Eilif and Morten shall see them every day, and when I die they shall be heirlooms. (*Poking under the bookcase.*) Hasn't—what the devil is her name?—the girl—hasn't she been for the glazier yet?

MRS. STOCKMANN (*coming in*). Yes, but he said he didn't know whether he'd be able to come to-day.

DR. STOCKMANN. You'll see he daren't come.

MRS. STOCKMANN. Well, Randine had an idea he was afraid to come, because of the neighbours.

(*Speaks through the sitting-room doorway.*) What is it, Randine?—All right. (*Goes out and returns immediately.*) Here's a letter for you, Thomas.

DR. STOCKMANN. Let's see. (*Opens the letter and reads.*) Aha!

MRS. STOCKMANN. Who's it from?

DR. STOCKMANN. From the landlord. He gives us notice.

MRS. STOCKMANN. Is it possible? Such a nice man as that——

DR. STOCKMANN (*looking at the letter*). He daren't do otherwise, he says. He's very loath to do it; but he daren't do otherwise—on account of his fellow-citizens—out of respect for public opinion—is in a dependent position—doesn't dare to offend certain influential men——

MRS. STOCKMANN. There, you see, Thomas.

DR. STOCKMANN. Yes yes, I see well enough; they're all cowards, every one of them, in this town; no one dares do anything for fear of all the rest. (*Throws the letter on the table.*) But it's all the same to us, Katrine. We'll be off to the new world, and then——

MRS. STOCKMANN. But are you sure this idea of going abroad is altogether wise, Thomas?

DR. STOCKMANN. Would you have me stay here where they have pilloried me as an enemy of the people, branded me, smashed my windows! And look here, Katrine, they've torn a hole in my black trousers.

MRS. STOCKMANN. Oh dear, and they're your best too!

DR. STOCKMANN. One should never put on his best trousers to go out to battle for freedom and truth. Of course, I don't care much about the trousers; you can always patch them up for me. But that the mob should dare to attack me as if they were my equals—*that's* what I can't stomach, for the life of me.

MRS. STOCKMANN. Yes, they've behaved abominably to you here, Thomas; but is that any reason for leaving the country altogether?

DR. STOCKMANN. Do you think the plebeians aren't just as insolent in other towns? Oh yes, they are, my dear; they're pretty much of a muchness everywhere. Well, never mind, let the curs snap; *that's* not the worst; the worst is that every one, all over the country, is the slave of his party. Not that I suppose—very likely it's no better in the free West either; the compact majority, and enlightened public opinion, and all the other devil's trash is rampant there too. But you see the conditions are larger there than here; they may kill you, but they don't slow-torture you; they don't put the screw on a free soul there, as they do at home here. And then, if need be, you can hold aloof from it all. (*Walks up and down.*) If I only knew of any primeval forest, or a little South Sea island to be sold cheap——

MRS. STOCKMANN. Yes, but the boys, Thomas.

DR. STOCKMANN (*comes to a standstill*). What an extraordinary woman you are, Katrine! Would you prefer the boys to grow up in such a society as ours? Why, you saw yourself yesterday evening that one-half of the population is stark mad, and if the other half hasn't lost its reason, that's only because they're hounds who haven't any reason to lose.

MRS. STOCKMANN. But really, my dear Thomas, you do say such imprudent things!

DR. STOCKMANN. Well, but isn't it the truth that I tell them? Don't they turn all ideas upside down? Don't they stir up right and wrong in one hotch-potch? Don't they call lies what I know to be truth? But the maddest thing of all is to see crowds of grown men, calling themselves Liberals, go about persuading themselves and others that they are friends of freedom! Did you ever hear anything like it, Katrine?

MRS. STOCKMANN. Yes, yes, no doubt it's all wrong together. But—— (PETRA *enters from the sitting-room.*) Back from school already?

PETRA. Yes; I've been dismissed.

MRS. STOCKMANN. Dismissed?

DR. STOCKMANN. You too!

PETRA. Mrs. Busk gave me notice, and so I thought it best to leave there and then.

DR. STOCKMANN. Quite right, my girl!

MRS. STOCKMANN. Who could have thought Mrs. Busk was such a bad woman?

PETRA. Oh mother, Mrs. Busk isn't bad at all; I saw clearly how much it pained her. But she didn't dare to do otherwise, she said; and so I'm dismissed.

DR. STOCKMANN (*laughing and rubbing his hands*). She dared not do otherwise. Just like the rest! Oh, it's delicious.

MRS. STOCKMANN. Oh well, after that frightful uproar last night——

PETRA. It wasn't only that. What do you think, father—— ?

DR. STOCKMANN. Well?

PETRA. Mrs. Busk showed me no fewer than three letters she had received this morning——

DR. STOCKMANN. Anonymous, of course?

PETRA. Yes.

DR. STOCKMANN. They've never the courage to give their names, Katrine——!

PETRA. And two of them stated that a gentleman who is often at our house said at the club last night that I held extremely advanced opinions upon various things——

DR. STOCKMANN. Of course you didn't deny it.

PETRA. Of course not. You know Mrs. Busk herself is pretty advanced in her opinions when we're alone together; but now that this has come out about me she dared not keep me on.

MRS. STOCKMANN. Some one that's often at our house, too! There, you see, Thomas, what comes of all your hospitality.

DR. STOCKMANN. We won't live any longer in such a pig-stye! Pack up as quickly as you can, Katrine; let's get away—the sooner the better.

MRS. STOCKMANN. Hush! I think there's some one in the passage. Just see, Petra.

PETRA (*opening the door*). Ah! is it you, Captain Horster? Please come in.

HORSTER (*from the anteroom*). Good morning. I thought I must just look in and see how you're getting on.

DR. STOCKMANN (*shaking his hand*). Thanks; that's very good of you.

MRS. STOCKMANN. And thanks for your escort home last night, Captain Horster.

PETRA. How did you ever get back again?

HORSTER. Oh, that was all right. You know I'm pretty strong, and those fellows' bark is worse than their bite.

DR. STOCKMANN. Isn't it marvellous, this piggish cowardice? Come here, I want to show you something! Look, here are all the stones they threw in at us. Only look at them! Upon my soul there aren't more than two decent-sized lumps in the whole heap; the rest are nothing but pebbles—mere gravel. They stood down there, and yelled, and swore they'd do me an injury;—but as for really doing it—no, there's mighty little fear of that in this town!

HORSTER. You may thank your stars for that this time, anyhow, Doctor.

DR. STOCKMANN. So I do, of course. But it's depressing all the same; for if it ever came to a serious national struggle, you'd see that public opinion would be for taking to its heels, and the compact majority would scamper for their lives like a flock of sheep, Captain Horster. That's what's so sad to think of; it grieves me to the heart.—But deuce take it—it's foolish of me to feel anything of the sort! They've called me an enemy of the people; well then, I'll *be* an enemy of the people!

MRS. STOCKMANN. That you'll never be, Thomas.

DR. STOCKMANN. You'd better not take your oath of it, Katrine. A bad name may act like a pin-scratch in the lung. And that confounded word—I can't get rid of it; it has sunk deep into my heart—and there it lies gnawing and sucking like an acid. And no magnesia can cure me.

PETRA. Pshaw! You should only laugh at them, father.

HORSTER. People will think differently yet, Doctor.

MRS. STOCKMANN. Yes, Thomas, that's as certain as that you're standing here.

DR. STOCKMANN. Yes, perhaps, when it's too late. Well, as they make their bed so they must lie! Let them go on wallowing here in the mire, and learn to repent having driven a patriot into exile. When do you sail, Captain Horster?

HORSTER. Hm—that's really what I came to speak to you about——

DR. STOCKMANN. Has anything gone wrong with the ship?

HORSTER. No; but the fact is, I'm not going with it.

PETRA. Surely you've not been dismissed?

HORSTER (smiling). Yes, I have.

PETRA. You too!

MRS. STOCKMANN. There, you see, Thomas.

DR. STOCKMANN. And for the truth's sake! Oh, if I could possibly have imagined such a thing——

HORSTER. You mustn't take it to heart; I shall soon get a berth with some other company, elsewhere.

DR. STOCKMANN. And this is Mr. Vik! A wealthy man, independent of any one! Good heavens——!

HORSTER. Oh, for that matter, he's a very well-meaning man ; and he says himself he would gladly have kept me on if only he dared.

DR. STOCKMANN. But he didn't dare—of course not!

HORSTER. It isn't easy, he says, when you belong to a party——

DR. STOCKMANN. My gentleman has hit it there! A party is like a sausage-machine; it grinds all the brains together in one mash; and that's why we see nothing but porridge-heads and pulp-heads all around!

MRS. STOCKMANN. Now really, Thomas!

PETRA (*to* HORSTER). If only you hadn't seen us home, perhaps it wouldn't have come to this.

HORSTER. I don't regret it.

PETRA (*gives him her hand*). Thank you for that!

HORSTER (*to* DR. STOCKMANN). What I wanted to say to you was this: if you're really determined to go abroad, I've thought of another way——

DR. STOCKMANN. That's good—if only we can get off——

MRS. STOCKMANN. Hush! Isn't that a knock?

PETRA. I'm sure that's uncle.

DR. STOCKMANN. Aha! (*Calls.*) Come in.

MRS. STOCKMANN. My dear Thomas, now do for once promise me——

(*The* BURGOMASTER *enters from the anteroom*).

BURGOMASTER (*in the doorway*). Oh! you're engaged. Then I'd better——

DR. STOCKMANN. No no; come in.

BURGOMASTER. But I wanted to speak with you alone.

MRS. STOCKMANN. We'll go into the sitting-room.

HORSTER. And I'll look in again presently.

DR. STOCKMANN. No no; go with the ladies, Captain Horster; I must have further information——

HORSTER. All right, then I'll wait.

(*He follows* MRS. STOCKMANN *and* PETRA *into the sitting-room. The* BURGOMASTER *says nothing, but casts glances at the windows.*)

DR. STOCKMANN. Perhaps you find it rather draughty here to-day? Put on your cap.

BURGOMASTER. Thanks, if I may (*does so*). I fancy I caught cold yesterday evening. I stood there shivering—

DR. STOCKMANN. Really? On my soul, I found it quite warm enough.

BURGOMASTER. I regret that it was not in my power to prevent these nocturnal excesses.

DR. STOCKMANN. Have you anything else in particular to say to me?

BURGOMASTER (*producing a large letter*). I have this document for you from the Directors of the Baths.

DR. STOCKMANN. I'm dismissed?

BURGOMASTER. Yes; from to-day. (*Places the letter on the table.*) We're very sorry—but, frankly, we dared not do otherwise on account of public opinion.

DR. STOCKMANN (*smiling*). Dared not? I've heard that phrase already to-day.

BURGOMASTER. I beg you to realise your position clearly. For the future, you can't count upon any sort of practice in the town.

DR. STOCKMANN. Deuce take the practice! But how can you be so sure of that?

BURGOMASTER. The Householders' Association is sending round a circular from house to house, in which all well-disposed citizens are called upon not to employ you; and I dare swear that not a single father of a family will venture to refuse his signature; he simply *dare* not.

DR. STOCKMANN. Well well; I don't doubt that. But what then?

BURGOMASTER. If I might advise you, I should say—leave the town for a time.

DR. STOCKMANN. Yes, I've been thinking of leaving the town.

BURGOMASTER. Good. And when six months or so have elapsed, if, after mature deliberation, you could make up your mind to acknowledge your error, with a few words of regret——

DR. STOCKMANN. I might perhaps be reinstated, you think?

BURGOMASTER. Perhaps; it's not quite out of the question.

DR. STOCKMANN. Yes, but how about public opinion? You daren't, on account of public opinion.

BURGOMASTER. Opinion is extremely variable. And, to speak candidly, it's of the greatest importance for us to have such an admission under your own hand.

DR. STOCKMANN. Then you may whistle for it! Surely you remember what I've said to you before about such foxes' tricks!

BURGOMASTER. At that time your position was infinitely more favourable; at that time you thought you had the whole town at your back——

DR. STOCKMANN. Yes, and now I've the whole town *on* my back—— (*Flaring up.*) But no—not if I had the devil and his dam on my back—never—never, I tell you!

BURGOMASTER. The father of a family has no right[1] to act as you are doing; you have no right to, Thomas.

DR. STOCKMANN. I have no right! There's only one thing in the world that a free man has no right to do; and do you know what that is?

BURGOMASTER. No.

DR. STOCKMANN. Of course not; but I'll tell you. A free man has no right to wallow in filth like a cur; he has no right to act so that he ought to spit in his own face.

BURGOMASTER. That sounds extremely plausible; and if there were not another explanation of your obstinacy—but we all know there is——

DR. STOCKMANN. What do you mean by that?

BURGOMASTER. You understand well enough. But as your brother, and as a man of common sense, I warn you not to build too confidently upon prospects and expectations that may very likely come to nothing.

---

[1] " Has no right " represents the Norwegian "tör ikke"—the phrase which, elsewhere in this scene, is translated "dare not." The latter rendering should perhaps have been adhered to throughout; but in this passage the Norwegian words convey a shade of meaning which is best represented by "has no right."—W. A.

DR. STOCKMANN. Why, what on earth are you driving at?

BURGOMASTER. Do you really want me to believe that you're ignorant of the terms of old Morten Kiil's will?

DR. STOCKMANN. I know that the little he has is to go to a home for old and needy artizans. But what's that got to do with me?

BURGOMASTER. To begin with, "the little he has" is no trifle. Morten Kiil is a tolerably wealthy man.

DR. STOCKMANN. I've never had the least notion of that——!

BURGOMASTER. Hm! Really? Then I suppose you had no notion that a not inconsiderable part of his fortune is to go to your children, you and your wife having a life-interest in it. Hasn't he told you that?

DR. STOCKMANN. No, on my soul! On the contrary, he's done nothing but grumble to me because he was so preposterously over-taxed. But are you really sure of this, Peter?

BURGOMASTER. I have it from a thoroughly trust-worthy source.

DR. STOCKMANN. Why, good heavens, then Katrine's safe!—and the children too! Oh! I must tell her—— (*Calls.*) Katrine, Katrine!

BURGOMASTER (*holding him back*). Hush! don't say anything about it yet.

MRS. STOCKMANN (*opening the door*). What is it?

DR. STOCKMANN. Nothing, my dear; go in again. (MRS. STOCKMANN *closes the door. He walks up and down.*) Provided for! Only think—all of them provided for! And for life! After all it's a blessed feeling to know that you're secure!

BURGOMASTER. Yes, but that's just what you're not. Morten Kiil can revoke his will any day or hour he chooses.

DR. STOCKMANN. But he won't, my good Peter. The Badger is only too delighted to see me attack you and your wiseacre friends.

BURGOMASTER (*starts and looks searchingly at him*). Aha! that throws a new light on a good many things.

DR. STOCKMANN. What things?

BURGOMASTER. So the whole affair has been a carefully concocted intrigue. Your recklessly violent onslaught—in the name of truth—upon the leading men of the town——

DR. STOCKMANN. Well, what of it?

BURGOMASTER. It was nothing but a preconcerted return for that vindictive old Morten Kiil's will.

DR. STOCKMANN (*almost speechless*). Peter—you're the most abominable plebeian I've ever known in my life.

BURGOMASTER. All is over between us. Your dismissal is irrevocable—for now we have a weapon against you.

(*He goes out.*)

DR. STOCKMANN. Shame! shame! shame! (*Calls.*) Katrine! The floor must be scrubbed after him! Tell her to come here with a pail—what's her name? confound it—the girl with the sooty nose——

MRS. STOCKMANN (*in the sitting-room doorway*). Hush, hush! Thomas!

PETRA (*also in the doorway*). Father, here's grandfather; he wants to know if he can speak to you alone.

DR. STOCKMANN. Yes, of course he can. (*By the door.*) Come in, father-in-law. (MORTEN KIIL *enters.* DR. STOCKMANN *closes the door behind him.*) Well, what is it? Sit down.

MORTEN KIIL. I won't sit down. (*Looking about him.*) It looks cheerful here to-day, Stockmann.

DR. STOCKMANN. Yes, doesn't it?

MORTEN KIIL. Sure enough it does; and you've plenty of fresh air too; you've surely got enough of that oxygen you were talking about yesterday. You must have an awfully good conscience to-day, I should think.

DR. STOCKMANN. Yes, I have.

MORTEN KIIL. So I should suppose. (*Tapping himself on the breast.*) But do you know what I've got here?

DR. STOCKMANN. A good conscience too, I hope.

MORTEN KIIL. Pshaw! No; something far better than that.

(*Takes out a large pocket-book, opens it, and shows* STOCKMANN *a bundle of papers.*)

DR. STOCKMANN (*looking at him in astonishment*). Shares in the Baths!

MORTEN KIIL. They weren't difficult to get to-day.

DR. STOCKMANN. And you've gone and bought these up——?

MORTEN KIIL. All I could possibly pay for.

DR. STOCKMANN. Why, my dear sir,—just when the Baths are in such a desperate condition——

MORTEN KIIL. If you behave like a reasonable creature, the Baths will soon be all right again.

DR. STOCKMANN. Well, you can see for yourself I'm doing all I can. But the people of this town are mad!

MORTEN KIIL. You said yesterday that the worst filth came from my tannery. Now, if that's true, then my grandfather, and my father before me, and I myself, have for ever so many years been poisoning the town, like three destroying angels. Do you think I'll sit quiet under such a reproach?

DR. STOCKMANN. Unfortunately, you can't help it.

MORTEN KIIL. No, thanks. I mean to stand up for my good name. I've heard that people call me "the Badger." Well, a badger's a sort of pig, I know; but I want to give them the lie. I will live and die a clean man.

DR. STOCKMANN. And how will you manage *that?*

MORTEN KIIL. You shall make me clean, Stock-mann.

DR. STOCKMANN. I!

MORTEN KIIL. Do you know with what money I've bought these shares? No, you can't know; but now I'll tell you. It's the money Katrine and Petra and the boys are to have after my death. For, you see, I've laid by something after all.

DR. STOCKMANN (*flaring up*). And you've taken Katrine's money for this!

MORTEN KIIL. Yes; the whole of it is invested in the Baths now. And now I want to see if you're

15

really stark, staring mad, Stockmann. If you go on making out that these beasts and other filthy things dribble down from my tannery, it'll be just as if you were to flay broad stripes of Katrine's skin—and Petra's too, and the boys. No decent father would ever do that—unless he were a madman.

DR. STOCKMANN (*walking up and down*). Yes, but I *am* a madman ; I *am* a madman !

MORTEN KIIL. You surely can't be so raving mad where your wife and children are concerned.

DR. STOCKMANN (*stopping in front of him*). Why couldn't you have spoken to me before you went and bought all that rubbish ?

MORTEN KIIL. What's done can't be undone.

DR. STOCKMANN (*walking restlessly about*). If only I weren't so certain about the affair——! But I'm absolutely convinced that I'm right !

MORTEN KIIL (*weighing the pocket-book in his hand*). If you stick to this madness, these aren't worth much.

(*Puts the book into his pocket.*)

DR. STOCKMANN. But, deuce take it ! surely science must be able to find some antidote, some sort of prophylactic——

MORTEN KIIL. Do you mean something to kill the animals ?

DR. STOCKMANN. Yes, or at least to make them harmless.

MORTEN KIIL. Can't you try rat's-bane ?

DR. STOCKMANN. Oh, nonsense, nonsense !— But since every one declares it's nothing but fancy, why fancy let it be ! Let them have their own way !

Haven't the ignorant, narrow-hearted curs reviled me as an enemy of the people?—and weren't they on the point of tearing the clothes off my back?

MORTEN KIIL. And they've smashed all your windows for you too!

DR. STOCKMANN. Then, too, one's duty to one's family! I must talk it over with Katrine; her judgment is so sound in matters of this sort.

MORTEN KIIL. That's right! You just follow the advice of a sensible woman.

DR. STOCKMANN (*going at him angrily*). How could you act so preposterously! Staking Katrine's money and getting me into this horrible dilemma! When I look at you, I seem to see the devil himself—— !

MORTEN KIIL. Then I'd better be off. But I must hear from you, yes or no, by two o'clock. If it's *no*, all the shares go to the Charity—and that this very day.

DR. STOCKMANN. And what does Katrine get?

MORTEN KIIL. Not a rap. (*The door of the anteroom opens.* HOVSTAD *and* ASLAKSEN *are seen outside it.*) Hullo! look at these two.

DR. STOCKMANN (*staring at them*). What! They actually dare to come here!

HOVSTAD. Why, of course we do.

ASLAKSEN. You see, we've something to say to you.

MORTEN KIIL (*whispers*). Yes or no—by two o'clock.

ASLAKSEN (*with a glance at* HOVSTAD). Aha!
    (MORTEN KIIL *goes out.*)

DR. STOCKMANN. Well, what do you want with me? Be brief.

HOVSTAD. I can well understand that you resent our conduct at the meeting yesterday——

DR. STOCKMANN. Your conduct, you say! Yes, it was pretty conduct! I call it misconduct—old-womanish cowardice. Shame upon you!

HOVSTAD. Call it what you will; but we *could* not act otherwise.

DR. STOCKMANN. You *dared* not, I suppose? Isn't that so?

HOVSTAD. Yes, if you like to put it that way.

ASLAKSEN. But why didn't you let us into the secret beforehand? Just the merest hint to Mr. Hovstad or to me?

DR. STOCKMANN. A hint? What about?

ASLAKSEN. About what was at the bottom of it.

DR. STOCKMANN. I don't in the least understand you.

ASLAKSEN (*nods confidentially*). Oh yes, you do, Dr. Stockmann.

HOVSTAD. It's no good making a mystery of it any longer.

DR. STOCKMANN (*looking from one to the other*). Why, what in the devil's name——!

ASLAKSEN. May I ask—isn't your father-in-law going about the town buying up all the shares in the Baths?

DR. STOCKMANN. Yes, he's been buying shares in the Baths to-day; but——

ASLAKSEN. It would have been more prudent to

let somebody else do that—some one not so closely connected with you.

HOVSTAD. And then you oughtn't to have appeared in the matter under your own name. No one need have known that the attack on the Baths came from you. You should have taken me into your counsels, Dr. Stockmann.

DR. STOCKMANN (*stares straight in front of him; a light seems to break in upon him, and he looks thunderstruck*). Is this possible? Can such things be?

ASLAKSEN (*smiling*). It's plain enough that they can. But they ought to be managed delicately, you understand.

HOVSTAD. And there ought to be other people in it; for the responsibility always falls more lightly when there are several to share it.

DR. STOCKMANN (*calmly*). In one word, gentlemen, what is it you want?

ASLAKSEN. Mr. Hovstad can best——

HOVSTAD. No, you explain, Aslaksen.

ASLAKSEN. Well, it's this: now that we know how the matter really stands, we believe we can venture to place the *People's Messenger* at your disposal.

DR. STOCKMANN. You can venture to now, eh? But how about public opinion? Aren't you afraid of bringing down a storm upon us?

HOVSTAD. We must manage to ride out the storm.

ASLAKSEN. And you must keep all your wits about you, Doctor. As soon as your attack has produced its effect——

DR. STOCKMANN. As soon as my father-in-law

and I have bought up the shares at a discount, you mean——?

HOVSTAD. No doubt it's mainly on scientific grounds that you want to take the management of the Baths into your own hands.

DR. STOCKMANN. Of course; it was on scientific grounds that I set the old Badger to work. And then we'll tinker up the water-works a little, and potter about a bit down at the beach, without its costing the town sixpence. Don't you think that'll do, eh?

HOVSTAD. I think so—if you have the *Messenger* to back you up.

ASLAKSEN. In a free society the press is a power, Doctor.

DR. STOCKMANN. Yes indeed, and so is public opinion; and you, Mr. Aslaksen—I suppose you'll be answerable for the Householders' Association?

ASLAKSEN. Both for the Householders' Association and the Temperance Society. You may rely upon that.

DR. STOCKMANN. But gentlemen—really I'm quite ashamed to mention such a thing—but—what return——?

HOVSTAD. Of course, we should prefer to give you our support for nothing. But the *Messenger* is not very firmly established; it's not getting on as it ought to; and I should be very sorry to have to stop the paper just now, when there's so much to be done in general politics.

DR. STOCKMANN. Naturally; that would be very hard for a friend of the people like you. (*Flaring up.*) But I—I am an enemy of the people!

(*Striding about the room.*) Where's my stick? Where the devil's my stick?

HOVSTAD. What do you mean?

ASLAKSEN. Surely you don't mean to——

DR. STOCKMANN (*standing still*). And suppose I don't give you a single farthing out of all my shares? You must remember we rich folk don't like parting with our money.

HOVSTAD. And *you* must remember that this business of the shares can be represented in two ways.

DR. STOCKMANN. Yes, you're the man for that; if I don't come to the rescue of the *Messenger*, you'll manage to put a vile complexion on the affair; you'll hunt me down, I suppose—bait me—try to throttle me as a dog throttles a hare.

HOVSTAD. That's a law of nature—every animal must fight for itself.

ASLAKSEN. And must take its food where it can find it, you know.

DR. STOCKMANN. Then see if you can't find some out in the gutter; (*striding about the room*) for now, by heaven! we'll see which is the strongest animal of us three. (*Finds his umbrella and brandishes it.*) Now, look here——!

HOVSTAD. You surely don't mean to assault us!

ASLAKSEN. I say, take care of that umbrella!

DR. STOCKMANN. Out at the window with you, Mr. Hovstad!

HOVSTAD (*by the anteroom door*). Are you quite mad?

DR. STOCKMANN. Out at the window, Mr. Aslaksen! Jump, I tell you! Be quick about it!

ASLAKSEN (*running round the writing-table*).
Moderation, Doctor; I'm delicate; I can't stand
much. (*Screams.*) Help! help!

(MRS. STOCKMANN, PETRA, *and* HORSTER *enter
from sitting-room.*)

MRS. STOCKMANN. Good heavens, Thomas!
what ever is the matter?

DR. STOCKMANN (*brandishing the umbrella*).
Jump, I tell you! Out into the gutter!

HOVSTAD. An unprovoked assault! I call you
to witness, Captain Horster.

(*Rushes off through the anteroom.*)

ASLAKSEN (*bewildered*). If one only knew the
local situation——!

(*He slinks out by the sitting-room door.*)

MRS. STOCKMANN (*holding back the* DOCTOR).
Now, do restrain yourself, Thomas!

DR. STOCKMANN (*throwing down the umbrella*). On
my soul, they've got off after all.

MRS. STOCKMANN. But what did they want with
you?

DR. STOCKMANN. I'll tell you afterwards; I've
other things to think of now. (*Goes to the table and
writes on a visiting-card.*) Look here, Katrine, what's
written here?

MRS. STOCKMANN. Three big *Noes;* what does
that mean?

DR. STOCKMANN. That I'll tell you afterwards, too.
(*Handing the card.*) There, Petra; let the girl run to
the Badger's with this as fast as she can. Be quick!

(PETRA *goes out through the anteroom with the
card.*)

DR. STOCKMANN. Well, if I haven't had visits to-day from all the emissaries of the devil! But now I'll sharpen my pen against them till it becomes a goad ; I'll dip it in gall and venom ; I'll hurl my ink-stand straight at their skulls.

MRS. STOCKMANN. Yes, but aren't we going away, Thomas?

(PETRA *returns.*)

DR. STOCKMANN. Well!

PETRA. All right.

DR. STOCKMANN. Good. Going away, do you say? No, I'll be damned if we do; we stay where we are, Katrine.

PETRA. Stay!

MRS. STOCKMANN. Here in the town?

DR. STOCKMANN. Yes, here; the field of battle is here; here the fight must be fought; here I will conquer! As soon as my trousers are mended, I'll go out into the town and look after a house; we must have a roof over our heads for the winter.

HORSTER. That you can have with me.

DR. STOCKMANN. Can I?

HORSTER. Yes, indeed you can. I've room enough, and, besides, I'm hardly ever at home.

MRS. STOCKMANN. Oh, how kind of you, Horster.

PETRA. Thank you.

DR. STOCKMANN (*shaking his hand*). Thanks, thanks! So that's off my mind. And this very day I shall set to work in earnest. Ah! there's a rare lot to be done here, Katrine! It's a good thing I've all my time at my disposal now; for you know I've had notice from the Baths——

MRS. STOCKMANN (*sighing*). Oh yes, I was expecting that.

DR. STOCKMANN. ——And now they want to take away my practice as well. But let them! The poor I shall keep anyhow—those that can't pay ; and, good Lord ! it's they that need me most. But by heaven ! I'll make them hear me ; I'll preach to them in season and out of season, as it's written somewhere.

MRS. STOCKMANN. My dear Thomas, I think you've seen what good preaching does.

DR. STOCKMANN. You really are ridiculous, Katrine. Am I to let myself be beaten off the field by public opinion, and the compact majority, and such devilry? No, thank you. Besides, my point is so simple, so clear and straightforward. I only want to drive into the heads of these curs that the Liberals are the worst foes of free men ; that party-programmes wring the necks of all young and vital truths ; that considerations of expediency turn justice and morality upside down, until life is simply hideous. Come, Captain Horster, don't you think I shall be able to make the people understand *that*?

HORSTER. Maybe ; I don't know much about these things myself.

DR. STOCKMANN. Well then—listen ! It's the party-leaders that must be got rid of. For, you see, a party-leader is just like a wolf—like a starving wolf ; he must devour a certain number of small animals a year, if he's to exist at all. Just look at Hovstad and Aslaksen ! How many small animals they polish off ; or else they mangle and maim them, so that they're fit for nothing else but to be house-holders and subscribers to the *People's Messenger.* (*Sits on the edge of the table.*) Just come here, Katrine; see how bravely the sun shines to-day! And how the blessed fresh spring air blows in upon me!

MRS. STOCKMANN. Yes, if only we could live on sunshine and spring air, Thomas!

DR. STOCKMANN. Well, you'll have to pinch and save where you can—and we'll get on all right. That's my least concern. Now what *does* trouble me is, that I don't see any man with enough independ-ence and nobility of character to dare to take up my work after me.

PETRA. Oh! don't bother about that, father; you have time before you.—Why, see, there are the boys already.

(EILIF *and* MORTEN *enter from the sitting-room.*)

MRS. STOCKMANN. Have you had a holiday to-day?

MORTEN. No; but we had a fight with the other fellows in play-time——

EILIF. That's not true; it was the other fellows that fought us.

MORTEN. Yes, and then Mr. Rörlund said we'd better stop at home for a few days.

DR. STOCKMANN (*snapping his fingers and spring-ing down from the table*). Now I have it, now I have it, on my soul! You shall never set foot in school again!

THE BOYS. Never go to school!

MRS. STOCKMANN. Why, Thomas——

DR. STOCKMANN. Never, I say. I'll teach you

myself—that's to say, I won't teach you any blessed thing——

MORTEN. Hurrah!

DR. STOCKMANN. —— ——but I'll try to make free, noble-minded men of you.—Look here, you'll have to help me, Petra.

PETRA. Yes father, you may be sure I will.

DR. STOCKMANN. And we'll have our school in the room where they reviled me as an enemy of the people. But we must have more pupils. I must have at least twelve boys to begin with.

MRS. STOCKMANN. You'll never get them in this town.

DR. STOCKMANN. We shall see! (*To the boys.*) Don't you know any street urchins—any regular ragamuffins——?

MORTEN. Yes father, I know lots!

DR. STOCKMANN. That's all right; bring me a few of them. I want to experiment with the street-curs for once; there are sometimes excellent heads among them.

MORTEN. But what are we to do when we've become free and noble-minded men?

DR. STOCKMANN. Drive all the wolves out to the far west, boys.

(EILIF *looks rather doubtful;* MORTEN *jumps about, shouting "Hurrah!"*)

MRS. STOCKMANN. If only the wolves don't drive you out, Thomas.

DR. STOCKMANN. Are you quite mad, Katrine! Drive *me* out! now that I'm the strongest man in the town!

MRS. STOCKMANN. The strongest—now?

DR. STOCKMANN. Yes, I venture to say this: that now I'm one of the strongest men upon earth.

MORTEN. I say, father!

DR. STOCKMANN (*in a subdued voice*). Hush! you mustn't speak about it yet; but I've made a great discovery.

MRS. STOCKMANN. What, again?

DR. STOCKMANN. Yes, certainly. (*Gathers them about him, and speaks confidentially.*) This is what I've discovered, you see: the strongest man upon earth is he who stands most alone.

MRS. STOCKMANN (*shakes her head, smiling*). Ah! Thomas——!

PETRA (*grasping his hands encouragingly*). Father!

OTHER WORKS BY
HENRIK IBSEN

Catiline (Catilina)

The Burial Mound Also Known As The Warrior's Barrow (Kjæmpehøjen)

Norma (Norma)

St. John's Eve (Sancthansnatten)

Lady Inger Of Oestraat (Fru Inger Til Østeraad)

The Feast At Solhaug (Gildet Paa Solhaug)

Olaf Liljekrans (Olaf Liljekrans)

The Vikings At Helgeland (Hærmændene Paa Helgeland)

Digte - Only Released Collection Of Poetry, Included "Terje Vigen"

Love's Comedy (Kjærlighedens Komedie)

The Pretenders (Kongs-Emnerne)

Brand (Brand)

Peer Gynt (Peer Gynt)

The League Of Youth (De Unges Forbund)

Emperor And Galilean (Kejser Og Galilæer)

Pillars Of Society (Samfundets Støtter)

A Doll's House (Et Dukkehjem)

Ghosts (Gengangere)

An Enemy Of The People (En Folkefiende)

The Wild Duck (Vildanden)

Rosmersholm (Rosmersholm)

The Lady From The Sea (Fruen Fra Havet)

Hedda Gabler (Hedda Gabler)

The Master Builder (Bygmester Solness)

Little Eyolf (Lille Eyolf)

John Gabriel Borkman (John Gabriel Borkman)

When We Dead Awaken (Når Vi Døde Vaagner)